Selected Poems

Kathleen Jamie

Selected Poems

PICADOR

First published 2018 by Picador
an imprint of Pan Macmillan
The Smithson, 6 Briset Street, London EC1M 5NR
EU Representative: Macmillan Publishers Ireland Limited,
1st Floor, The Liffey Trust Centre, 117-126 Sheriff Street Upper, Dublin, D01 YC43

Associated companies throughout the world
www.panmacmillan.com

ISBN 978-1-5098-8295-3

Printed and bound in Great Britain by TJ Books Limited, Padstow, Cornwall

Visit **www.picador.com** to read more about all our books
and to buy them. You will also find features, author interviews and
news of any author events, and you can sign up for e-newsletters
so that you're always first to hear about our new releases.

To the memory of Isabel and Bob Jamie

– Mum and Dad

Contents

[ix]

[xi]

From BLACK SPIDERS
(1982)

Black Spiders

He looked up to the convent
she'd gone to. She answered no questions
but he knew by the way she'd turned away
that morning.
He felt like swimming to the caves.

*

The nuns have retreated. The eldest still
peals the bell in glee, although no one comes
from the ruins. All their praying was done
when they first saw the ships and the Turks'
swords reflecting the sun.

In the convent the cistern is dry,
the collection boxes empty – cleft skulls
severed and bleached,
are kept in a shrine, and stare to the East.

*

She caught sight of him later, below, brushing salt
from the hair of his nipples. She wanted them
to tickle; black spiders on her lips.

Women in Jerusalem

'Alo! Germanee? Welcome! Alo! America?'
I hid from the spat crudities of Arabs,
the continuous stare, unblinking sun,
in a crumbling dorm all hanging with garments.
A drowsy voice asked 'Alo, Englis?'
We were instantly friends.

In the market we discussed wares
in gobbledegook for the sake of peace.
We talked, in the shade of the hostel,
of the world's brute men, money, politics
and the good things of home.

On the balcony we sat above the flies,
the broad mules' backs, brown Bedouin hands
weighing and arguing figs; she spat
an insect from her fingers, handed money
to her husband. I saw a man
at the Damascus Gate, and cursed.

Obscured now and then by women in abayehs,
shaped like barrels and walking as barrels
would, hooped with belts. I was sure.
My friend peeped out. I was purdah'd: the door
opened into his view. We conferred like Arab sisters.

'I'd invited him to Massada, and split.
We don't understand each other
at all. "I," he said, "protect you."
From whom? He shrugged "It's our mentality".
I went alone:

On the plain in the haze the road is laid down
like an almighty crucifixion. At the junction
a fat hand twists my wrist. He offers
200 shequel, kaffiyas, toy camels,
the sundry geegaws of his stall and
a lift to Jerusalem.

His son watches and learns, and lets
ecstatic flies crawl over a scab in his ear.
There is dust; a mirage of a bus, a
sign of life. I run . . .'

We'd been under siege all afternoon,
telling tales, occasionally checking
and ducking. Neighbouring roofs
were reconnoitred for routes.
He expected my pale bare flesh
to mark me out, and sat tight.
We gave in towards night.

In the room were foul and ancient abaheys,
we hooped them round and laughed at ourselves.
They blacked out the sound of our voices
and hid our bodies from sight.

The Barometer

Last year
Mother threw the barometer
the length of the corridor. This:
she has set her jaw. There's a chill
and the rustle of weeds. She's come in
from the garden, now she'll withdraw.

The maids are shivering. Outside
they're talking of snow. I say no
to a fire – it's an act of surrender.

I can see the bare fields from here
on the balcony. The nights
are growing longer. I know.
At least the harvest is gathered and safe.
– Every thanksgiving
I dance like a Romany. Indian summers;
I giggle and weep. Mother and me
go picnics in the blossoming . . .

My furs are laid out and waiting.
The maids keep tutting.
I catch myself biting
dead skin from my lips.
I have played with my gloves all day.

I ought just to jump
and meet Hades half way.

The Harbour

At the centre, red and dripping
are wreckers' lights. By night
they await the occasional drift, but gallop
away at the fall of day, frustrated
by sure navigation and calm.

The harbour could be anywhere.
In its wall are a window, a board and door;
the home of a hermit whose
nights and days are tidal,
his house being rhythmically drowned.

On the board are meticulous notes,
on the rising and settling of waves,
his service to fishers and curious tourists:
only the price of paper – like this –
is requested and paid.

The dock where vessels leave is walked
by a resentful temptress who shrieks
if she catches you staring away from her legs.
She says she finds hammers
better than lovers.

Back country is as yet unexplored. They say
the sky is the colour of bruise. The sun:
underground. Rocks glow like night-lights
with the strain of containing it

Inhumation

No one knows if he opened his eyes,
acknowledged the dark,
felt around, found and drank
the mead provided, supposing himself
dead.

Storm in Istanbul

Beware the temper of the only god.
We asked only rain to smother the dust.

By three we'd kicked off the single grey sheet.
The patrol passed in the alley.

We took it for a torch, a search, we could not speak
above the roar, we opened a window
and heard the boots. Leaned out, tongues out
to taste the rain.

In the flash you could read the armoured car's plate.
The guard saw moving shapes, fired
shouts between the cracking of petrified cloud.
He laughed too loud when
he linked arms with his chum
('Thought you was a terrorist, didn'I?')
Their uniforms scraped.

You could have shot him from here,
some mother's gaunt son. Not even having
his big boots on could save him
from flinching when his almighty blue mosque
was lit from above.
He crouched below his bayonet. It gleamed
like the minarets jabbing the sky
that shuddered and roared in pain.

Beside the rancid heap where it eats a dog wept.
All the cats howled. It gave him
the creeps. He whispered through his teeth
to calm them. For him
someone began to play a pipe,
a few shaking voices sang. Light was coming . . .

From the towers came the wail of a failing old imam.

The faithful went to pray.
The heathen, we slept.

Permanent Cabaret

Our highwire artiste,
knowing nothing of fear, will take
sparkling risks fifty feet high.
Her costume, ladies, is iced with
hard diamonds.
While she mounts all those steps
our old friend the clown will stand
upside down in a shower of confetti
and chirp 'Love me!'

Their lamp is the last on camp to go out.
Coco reads Jung, sometimes aloud to
Estelle, if she's sewing on sequins.
More often she practises alone in the ring
for the day she enters permanent cabaret,
perhaps in Zurich. Coco cracks his knuckles,
thinking vaguely of children, or considers
repainting the outside of their van.

Half way across Estelle glitters like frost.
She has frozen. 'Remain professional.' She
draws breath through her teeth, wavers
her hand: 'Let Coco sense something for once!'
His red boots are edging towards her. He
coaxes, offers aid – his absurd umbrella.
The audience wonder: is it part of the show
this embarrassing wobbling,
this vain desperation to clutch?

From THE WAY WE LIVE
(1987)

Julian of Norwich

Everything I do I do for you.
Brute. You inform the dark
inside of stones, the winds draughting in

from this world and that to come,
but never touch me.
You took me on

but dart like a rabbit into holes
from the edges of my sense
when I turn, walk, turn.

*

I am the hermit whom you keep
at the garden's end, but I wander.
I am wandering in your acres

where every step, were I
attuned to sense them,
would crush a thousand flowers.

(Hush, that's not the attitude)
I keep prepared a room and no one comes.
(Love is the attitude)

*

Canary that I am, caged and hung
from the eaves of the world
to trill your praise.

He will not come.
Poor bloodless hands, unclasp.
Stiffened, stone-cold knees, bear me up.

(And yet, and yet, I am suspended
in his joy, huge and helpless
as the harvest moon in a summer sky.)

Peter the Rock

The last trumpet of sunlight blows over the sea,
he moves high on the cliff, sure of his grace
and raises an arm. The fingers connect.
He pulls up and leans out, hair falling straight toward earth.

He tells me he dreams about nothing
but falling, though we sleep on the sand.
His arms always round me, golden hair
spilled over my face. That mysterious injury
torn in his shoulders: 'I told you, I fell.'

Even in kissing you feel for holds,
grip through to bone.
It doesn't surprise me, I do it myself,
enrage you with symbol, the meaning of things.
You practise moves and hate gestures,
God-talk with vengeance, imperfect shoulders.

I change the tapes. He drives, and will go on denying
into the night. There is nothing
but rock and the climbing of rock under the sun.
Which I say is falling and setting behind us, unfolded,
flashed in the wing mirrors, golden, your skin tone.

from Karakoram Highway

4

At the sharp end of the gorge;
the bridge. Like a single written word
on vast and rumpled parchment. Bridge.
The statement of man in landscape.

And how they guard it.
Drifts of people in either bank
like brackets, knowing it can crash
to the river in a mangled scribble
and be erased.
They write it up again, single syllable
of construction
shouted over the canyon.

5

And all the driver wants is eye-drops
before he straightens up the bus, commits us.
At least malevolence concedes your existence;
worse is indifference, power and indifference.
The river brawls beneath us, self-obsessed,
narcissistic. Wheels turn, turn again, full weight.
The bridge starts to undulate and we're hanging
out of windows half-roads over the Indus,

grinning at each other, impotent, enlightened.
The world grew tight.

It must have been about then we first saw the mountains.

6

Emotion is human, the foothills brown,
the valley floor very low. We haven't slept.
Our thoughts are slow and wide.
The mind can turn its own death in its hand,
chat blythly about mountains, until
the last moment, that appalling rise that ends
in total unemotional blue.
First sight of the summits, distant
and almost transparent, like glass.
Call it distance, not menace. White, not frightening:
emotion is human, is returned to the human
along with your life. A slight
clash of terror, you lower your eyes.
The sun reflected from glass,
more fearsome than glass in itself.

7

It's earthly and brown, deep inside canyons.
Stones at the roadside:
'Here rock fell on men', 'men fell to the river'

and the river and rock were unmoved
being river and rock.
He takes it fast.
Some nameless white mountain
has closed off the end of the canyon.
The walls grow taller, the river hysterical.
He brakes, hauls the wheel. No talking.
No colour but brown –
except in the mind. It's been many hours.
Fear passes out into long passive blue,
a slight smile – there is nothing at all we can do.
And the sky widens, the canyon gives out
to a strange sort of kingdom
and the first hanging village swings in.

8

The year's greening crop spilled
down dull unaltering rock like the tail
of a bird. We can recognise this:

that crops yellow, get cut,
turn in on themselves over winter, head under wing,
and begin to feel like ourselves again.

Suspended villages, terraces
layered wide in the movement of scythes,
the unthreatening gesture of sowing.

9

Maybe this is as close as we'll get to the mountains.

Squatting on the steps of the K2 Motel
another wretched K2 cigarette.
No great altitude. Clouds sit like headaches
on the walls of this desolate vast arena,
gather round like the Skardu men
with chapati-hats, their clothes
come through dust-storms down the bazaar.

Someone's cooking. The bus has turned back.
Silence and space fall strangely on us all;
leaned against walls with the gear.
Some look at the finances, some at a half-baked
patch of grass, waiting for food
and the day after tomorrow.

Some just look at the hills, keep looking,
tapping plastic spoons onto plastic plates.

Aunt Janet's Museum

What can be gained by rushing these things?
Huddle in from the rain, compose ourselves, let
a forefinger rest on the bell button which
requests kindly 'p   s'. We wait, listening
to bus tyres on rain say *hush* and *west*.
People hurry behind us, we wait,
for shuffling inside the door,
tumbling locks, and admission to dark.

One after the other we make up the stair.
No one looks back, we know what's there,
fear what lies ahead may disappear. Could we
forget these ritual sounds, or alter their order?
Scuffle of feet on the narrow stair,
the alcove, the turn where
pallid light faints through the glass of the doors.

Let it be right. She takes the handle, still
softly exclaiming over our height, and lets her weight
drop it. The click of the latch. She pushes the door
till the shop bell above gives a delicate ting.
Sounds of inside step forward. The faraway drill
of bells warning the kitchen, and the fallible clock.

The Way We Live

Pass the tambourine, let me bash out praises
to the Lord God of movement, to Absolute
non-friction, flight, and the scarey side:
death by avalanche, birth by failed contraception.
Of chicken tandoori and reggae, loud, from tenements,
commitment, driving fast and unswerving
friendship. Of tee-shirts on pulleys, giros and Bombay,
barmen, dreaming waitresses with many fake-gold
bangles. Of airports, impulse, and waking to uncertainty,
to strip-lights, motorways, or that pantheon –
the mountains. To overdrafts and grafting

and the fit slow pulse of wipers as you're
creeping over Rannoch, while the God of moorland
walks abroad with his entourage of freezing fog,
his bodyguard of snow.
Of endless gloaming in the North, of Asiatic swelter,
to launderettes, anecdotes, passions and exhaustion,
Final Demands and dead men, the skeletal grip
of government. To misery and elation; mixed,
the sod and caprice of landlords.
To the way it fits, the way it is, the way it seems
to be: let me bash out praises – pass the tambourine.

From THE AUTONOMOUS REGION
(1993)

1

O a great downward lurch of the heart, as though
he dreamily stepped off an unexpected kerb;
Fa-hsien in the city. He says:
> '*Need all situations be resolvable/ resolved?'*
or
> '*Is* there a high pass over the mountains?'

and hopes/hopes not. Rumour flits the city
like bats, flits the city like bats by night,
rumours on the lips of running tea-boys,
delivered on the hour, on trays like tea.
> And the rumours say yes, the rumours say no.

And with a great shout and a creak
the shoulders of 100 youths
pulled the wingèd city gates, and all
that were going walked or rode
out to the desert before them.

2

Fires burning in the bellies of yurts at the day's end:
beside a river, such a clear stream there, with a fish.
If he could return he'd return to that river
as the sun rose like a fish behind mountains
and the stream, cleared to crystal, foretold.
A purple range to East and to West,
he remarks:

                'Not a few have turned back.
Promise or rumour without author or source
ever keeps us moving, against the way
of the small clear river' – which is to say: uphill.
Devotions over, the ice mountains'
jagged edges met his gaze. He smiles, 'Life!
Wo! *That* straggling caravan.' Then: 'But what to you
are the ramblings of Fa-hsien?' Begins to walk.

3

Walked beneath the power lines
(sagging like pigs' bellies in the sun)
between the desert graves and gravel mounds,
scared the crows with open black beaks, walked
abandoned tar-barrels, wiped the sweat
and wondered aloud:

                              'How did this begin?'
just one tiny act: he'd dropped the keys back
thro' the letter-box.
And though molten tar got stuck to his feet,
all in all he thought it rather wonderful.
He said to himself:

                              'Well, is there?'
when, to others insisted:

                              'There *is*.' Secretly, he loved
the way his lips cracked, loved
to feel his head spin, loved
to cough the dust and consider himself
a journeyman, a-journeying.

4

Meanwhile, in another place,
the princess (travelling, travelling)
breaks the Sun-Moon Mirror and weeps.

A strong-willed woman and resolute,
she knows when to weep.

5 *The princess breaks the Sun-Moon Mirror*

As if a city child knows his heart
can take no more of this awful thudding,
and in a cellar stale and hot,
black and breathy
as his granny's lap
escapes his mother's grasp
and makes by alleys and deserted wynds
to the splintering gates,
hears the roar, knows all's lost
                    so opens them.
                            'What I will I own' says the princess.
                            Surveys her perfect world.
                            A life thrown round my shoulders
                            luxurious as fur; my heart twitches
                            like a dreaming cat.'
Dear maid running
with sodden clothes clung to her like children
whose rain-soaked face is like a sister's,
whose company is a clear pool
on a deep and secret river
grasp each other horrified as flowers
and cannot even yell above the wind
sees the mirror smashed at the princess' tiny feet
and on her lips
the beginnings
of a terrible
and mischievous
smile.

6

Carved dragons framed the door, fierce and delicate
our house-on-stilts. Creepers chased like monkeys
round our high, half-hidden walls whose gates
opened onto tree-tops; streams
flashing to the village pleased us first. I loved
the tremors that occasionally bucked
our youthful gorge as if a finger
traced its spine. My colour then
was mother-of-pearl; my bed and bedding,
nails, the combs that held my ornate hair . . .
I'd lean on the verandah, breathe jasmine
air, lean on the verandah, lean and fancy.
But I loved it best when snow came, the distant world
would soothe its troubled self into a pearl.

7

'The shattered windscreen splits the sun
to a glass chrysanthemum. A few dead buildings
the road's cast up like shells. Your turn.'
'There's nothing here for us,
just a couple of nomads' yurts. Darling
this is *gulag*.' Wen Cheng
chucked a bottle from the window,
watched it splash to bits with a certain
satisfaction. 'What,' she asked
'are those sacks out there,
ranked like the dumb soldiers of the terracotta army?'
(those that were new were full of desert dust,
those that were old had rot)
'It's the labour of the people,' said the maid
and lit a cigarette.

8

After three days in the desert he came to a spring.
Laughing, grins, 'sweat, mortals, crowd
like wing-torn moths about me'; it was
all charm, the winning smile, laughed
until it fell away in channels; the channels
run to villages, are disciples with news
of glories and miracles sparkling on their lips.
Harvests are delivered fathered by disciples.
For a short time he took this in.
                    Then it was back to the desert.

Sits a lassie in red scarf,
wi her heid in her hauns, her heid
achin wi the weicht o so much saun
the weicht o the desert that waits every morn
an blackly dogs her back.

And road-builders watch their passing, turn
like weary sunflowers tracking the sun.

9

So said the maid into her dictaphone:
'Times she'd sit and hum discordant notes
above her walkman, growl
"I'm drowning in this desert" another hour
and she'd mutter:
                    a girl
                            could get
                                    bored.'

Wen Cheng's
            acting up, yes
she's wilding in the dining-car
I hear the
            smash of crockery, the waiter
swirling like a matador and fair enough
it's 2 a.m. (Beijing). Now comes she lurching:
'Pass the phrase-book, darling,
let's have a sesh with these dear Uygar boys.'
The Uygar stare at this phenomenon, but
they've tired of their comic books,
give toothless grins and pass the bottle.

So the train bends on. Come the day
the boys and her still playing
paper/stone/knife to some serious arak.
It's a lengthy journey, it's a battlefield;
sprawling bodies stir and find their
rightful owners. A hard-bit woman
sweeps the husks and fag-ends out onto the track.

The princess rises with all her grace and lurches

down the corridor, the boys discuss
in guttural tongues. She's back:
this time announced
'It's not unusual for golden-hairs
to lie where
Chinese only spit.' '?' I said
'Read it some place,' she replied and
took another swig. Her last.'

The party journeyed on for 15 days
in a south-westerly direction
over a difficult, precipitous and dangerous
road, the side of the mountain
being like a stone wall
10,000 feet in height.

10

Unbeknown to them, Fa-hsien,
riding hobo on the box-car
sees the desert change miraculous to plain.
He fancies in the sheep-dogs' bark
a hidden 'yes!' and doesn't half
admire how the nomads ride,
so splits his time, between, on one hand,
attending to the scenery
he's dragged across,
and on the other, learning to divine.

Learning to divine his own future.
He's laying low, he's two days out
heart-in-mouth and hiding from the police
and diesel fumes. It's a truck-of-lead
and slow. The sky's detonated
blue across the day; he stares it out
and hopes, conversely fears and knows.
He feels quite sick. It's worth it.

Swags and swathes of hills billowing o
as a child he dreamed of sailing; the sailing hills;
he hears his heart shanty and shepherds
call like bosuns.

The prayer-flags yearn like full-rigged ships
to quit this witness, earth. He knows
already he's too far slipped
to make the leap ashore.
Aye, it's strange quiver; and he knows
himself an arrow already shot the bow.
He cries, tells himself, as if he didn't know
It's worth it, worth it, worth it.

11 *The travels of Fa-hsien*

His bed is hard, his smell
a travel-musk of months through teeming villages.
The walls of course are stained, the sheet
he almost envies: old, plain.

He rises, ties his top-knot,
wanders to the boiler-room, with his
double-happiness thermos flask,
noting
      every vessel can be broken, filled,
and he's empty, these days. Not old
as the sun-lines round his eyes suggest
which eyes have seen:
        many things out of strong places
et cetera. And who knows what his robe conceals:
tattoos, a bleeding heart.

*

There's roads and there are one-horse-towns
and any climb out of hamlet, gorge or wilderness
he looks in wonder,
to fellow travellers he replies:
'What wisdom have I gathered? None!
That's my tuppence worth', walks on. 'Threw it in a ditch and
    walk unburdened.'

And also in the ditch, a dog, days dead, ignored.
'I've lied and vowed at umpteen altars,
and know I can be
                    utterly deceived.
Perhaps still am.'

At the thin black line of shade at a truckstop
while they fix the fan-belt
and there's no water
he'll bring out yarrow-stalks, divine.
And sometimes, walking alone, he finds
the centre of his being, flinches,
for it's nowt
              but an alms bowl.
Waiting at a roadside, he scratches the dust
with a stick, finds: more dust.
In the hot shade of some godforsaken Xinjiang bunkhouse
remembers the river and the fish.

(o monk, whither do you wander?
to garner wisdom and bring scripture home)

12

Fine horsewomen both and a long time travelling.
Wen Cheng bends low and adjusts the stirrup.
Something tells her this is the border: a breath of wind
from the dark and jagged mountains
a circus of secrets in the valley at her feet.

Nights, and the tents glow in a river bend,
the keepers of secrets
                together in cliques –
master brewers growing merry round a camp-fire;
thin-faced glass-makers trickle silt
                    between their fingers,
the silk-workers guard their covered baskets.
And Wen Cheng could read the marks of darkness.
O rumour, they have no paper, beer, script.
Sometimes she wonders
                what kind of place it is she's going,
kicks the horse and turns down before nightfall.

Like the others these days she talks most about the future;
out in the night they're starting to communicate;
secrets revealed and revealed amongst themselves.

We crossed the watershed. A small stream
ran with us down the mountain;
a thumb of rainbow marked the sky.
At the doors of yurts
women and girls wiped their brows
and waved as they churned
summer to its yellow end, a sound
like oars
                on a still and distant loch.

In a purse the mirror's shards
tied from her waist, tinkled most attractively
as we rode; smashed, she sighed
            into this/ not this
            like a common
                bottle
                of bitter beer.

And holding the dancing horse on a tight rein
twisted back, hair joyously undone
I told her 'we are tense vessels, each contain
all the energy required for change'
which made her laugh, and I knew
that if her robes indeed concealed
            a little lady's
          pearl-handled pistol
it was for nought
but shooting locks off boxes, prison cells et cetera.

As yaks gathered at the fanks,
like an inhaled breath, buttercups
at their patient hooves
hardened their hearts
against the night. Our running dogs
sniffed a hint of snow,
on the golden sunset
where a lark's black flight
leapt and leapt
like a telegraph wire
on a straight road.

At the shore of a loch called Qinghai we rested,
hobbled the horses and let them graze
the sweet wild pasture.

13

Fa-hsien, cross-legged in a light rain,
takes his tin spectacle case,
    watches the first print he ever made
(on a lonely shore)
              wash away.
Though desert dust still clings to his hems
he has bathed fresh and clean
in his joyous lake,
and now his hand and cards have changed,
reveal
a hanker for his ain folk,
        his auld hert follows suit.

14

When we reached the lake, pure and shining,
like a mirror of itself
in sheer joy we jumped down, swirled round and round
so our clothes belled out and graced the silt
with a circle which we defined:
Our space
Mine
which I hadn't done since we were bairns
in gym-shoes.

(and I recalled the last town we'd passed,
en fête, where jugglers and acrobats
called a crowd around
but its centre was their stage.
In that dirty township
     I hid my face
behind a fluttering fan,
of Queens and Aces,
so by the angry hiss of a
hurricane lamp
in the back of a chop-house
lost and won a pretty sum
and some I tossed to a blind beggar,
some a pick-pocket filched
and three gold coins I saved
for out the corner
    of my eye,

behind my winning hand I'd seen
a wandering holy-man and part-time diviner.

Whose little fire rose scented
Smoke into the sky, along the shore.

The joyous lake

turned coral, jasper in the gloaming,
a heron beat its languid wings,
though he called them back, shore-birds
flashed, were gone;

a woman in silhouette
arranged some silvered shards
on a granite boulder
then played a reed pipe
over the water

and with these folk Fa-hsien
devoured a meal,
shared travellers' nonsense,
risqué jokes,

Then I asked:
will we come this way again, this smiling lake?
And though the princess laid off playing
turned her back, we could feel
she was all ears when he warned
some things may never be resolved
then studied my upturned hand.

My cross-hatched palm: lines straight
as a cormorant's flight
                       like an arrow shot
slow over the silent loch

said all that was past was lost
and there was everything to come

grew serious
as bracken shook, horses stamped the troubled loch sent waves ashore,

Set a stout hert tae a stey brae
           he winked (a wink that showed
he wasn't so old he couldn't
follow home a twisting road
with a click of his heels,
wouldn't resist
             a backward glance
to see who followed this ridiculous dance
through many people's many tongues.)

∧

A sharp and sudden wind
forced between loch and sky
as if from under an ill-fitting door

as the princess tossed the coins
through heads and tails

and even she who'd snorted 'truth?
a game of spot-the-ball'

grew serious
as bracken shook, horses stamped
the troubled loch sent waves ashore,

scattered the diviner's cards,
our faces there.

Calm: and Fa-hsien took a twig
drew in the dust the coins' revelation

spoke to a place at the centre of us all:
the fire's core,

described a future in a measured tone:
if she'd be true

to her mirror
cracked, her inner loch, that humble heart,

the great force of that keen wind: her name
would be revered.

*

15

We saw him once more: in the dusty dawn
a distant home-turned figure
jaunty as a fiddler
down the loch-side dirt track.

As we saddled up, ready for the last push,
wondering again what kind of place it was
we rode toward
                        with a new resolve.

18 For Paola

A boomin echo doon the corridor,
her door's the only ane open

lik a shell, an a wumman sweepin:
saft soun, wings.

A licht-bulb, hingit fi the ceiling
by a short cord.

A slever o gless in the oose
an a black hair. she telt me

they've killed 5000 people in Beijing.
Nou this wumman's haunin her gear

brushes an pens, her worn claes
for me tae cairry. But she'd a bin waitin

when they cam, chewin her gum
blawn them a bubble size o China.

This is a place your friens disappear:
trust naebody. Luve a.

The smearit wa's o a concrete room,
a wumman sweepin.

20 *Xiahe*

Abune the toon o Xiahe
a thrast monastery,
warn lik a yowe's tuith.

The sun gawps at innermaist
ingles o wa's.
Secret as speeders

folk hae criss-crosst a saucht
seedt i the yird flair
wi rags o win blawn prayer.

Xiahe. Wave droonin wave
on a pebbly shore,
the *ahe* o machair, o slammach,

o impatience; ahent the saft saltire
i trashed, an sheep;
wha's drift on the brae

is a lang cloud's shadda.
the herd cries a wheen wirds
o Tibetan sang,

an A'm waukenet, on a suddenty mindit:
A'm far fae hame,
I hae crossed China.

Xiahe (pronounced *Shi-ah-e*) a Tibetan town in the now Chinese province of Gansu; **sauch**: willow; **yird**: earth; **slammach**: cobweb.

From THE QUEEN OF SHEBA
(1994)

The Queen of Sheba

Scotland, you have invoked her name
just once too often
in your Presbyterian living rooms.
She's heard, yea
even unto heathenish Arabia
your vixen's bark of poverty, come down
the family like a lang neb, a thrawn streak,
a wally dug you never liked
but can't get shot of.

She's had enough. She's come.
Whit, tae this dump? Yes!
She rides first camel
of a swaying caravan
from her desert sands
to the peat and bracken
of the Pentland hills
across the fit-ba pitch
to the thin mirage
of the swings and chute; scattered with glass.

Breathe that steamy musk
on the Curriehill Road, not mutton-shanks
boiled for broth, nor the chlorine stink
of the swimming pool where skinny girls
accuse each other of verrucas.

In her bathhouses women bear
warm pot-bellied terracotta pitchers
on their laughing hips.
All that she desires, whatever she asks
She will make the bottled dreams
of your wee lasses
look like *sweeties*.

Spangles scarcely cover
her gorgeous breasts, hanging gardens
jewels, frankincense; more voluptuous
even than Vi-next-door, whose
high-heeled slippers
keeked from dressing gowns
like little hooves, wee tails
of pink fur stuffed in the cleavage of her toes;
more audacious even than Currie Liz
who led the gala floats
through the Wimpey scheme
in a ruby-red Lotus Elan
before the Boys' Brigade band
and the Brownies' borrowed coal-truck;
hair piled like candy-floss;
who lifted her hands from the neat wheel
to tinkle her fingers
at her tricks

    among the Masons and the elders and the police.

The cool black skin
of the Bible couldn't hold her,
nor the atlas green
on the kitchen table,
you stuck with thumbs
and split to fruity hemispheres –
yellow Yemen, Red Sea, *Ethiopia*. Stick in
with the homework and you'll be
cliver like yer faither,
but no too cliver,
no *above yersel*.

See her lead those great soft camels
widdershins round the kirk-yaird,
smiling
as she eats
avocados with apostle spoons
she'll teach us how. But first

she wants to strip the willow
she desires the keys
            to the National Library

she is beckoning
      the lasses
      in the awestruck crowd . . .

Yes, we'd like to
            clap the camels,
to smell the spice,
admire her hairy legs and
bonny wicked smile, we want to take
PhDs in Persian, be vice
to her president: we want
to help her
        ask some Difficult Questions

she's shouting for our wisest man
to test her mettle:

            Scour Scotland for a Solomon!

Sure enough: from the back of the crowd
someone growls:
                whae do you think y'ur?

and a thousand laughing girls and she
draw our hot breath
            and shout:

THE QUEEN OF SHEBA!

Mother-May-I

Mother-May-I
go down the bottom of the lane,
to the yellow-headed piss-the-beds,
and hunker at the may-hedge, skirts
fanned out
             in the dirt and see the dump
where we're not allowed –
twisty trees, the burn, and say:
      all hushed sweetie-breath:
      they are the woods
where men
             lift up your skirt
and take down your pants
even although you're crying.
Mother may I
             leave these lasses' games
                   and play at Man-hunt, just
in the scheme Mother
may I
   tell small lies: *we were sot*
in the lane, sat on garage ramps,
picking harling
with bitten nails, as myths
rose thick as swamp mist
from the woods behind the dump
                   where hitch-hikers rot
in the curling roots of trees.

and men
leave tight rolled-up
dirty magazines.
Mother may we

         pull our soft backsides
through the jagged may's
white blossom, run across the stinky dump
and muck about
at the woods and burn
             dead pleased
to see the white dye
of our gym-rubbers seep downstream?

A Shoe

On the dry sand of Cramond I found
    a huge
        platform sole, a wedge
of rubber gateau among the o-so
rounded pebbles
        the occasional
washed up san-pro.

I could arrange it in the bathroom
with the pretty
        Queeny shells, God,
we'd laugh, wouldn't we, girls?

        Those bloody bells
ringing down corridors
hauling us this way and that;
    wee sisters and pals
      tugging our hair,
        folders, books
and those shoes – stupid
as a moon walker's; ah,
      the comfort of gravity.

You don't suppose she just
        stepped off the Forth Bridge,
head over heels, shoes self-righting
      like a cat.

hair and arms flying up
    as she slid down through the water?

Or did she walk in, saying yes
        I recognise this
as the water yanked heavy
    on thighs belly breasts?

God girls, we'd laugh:
        it's all right once you're in.
it's all right
        once you're out the other side.

Hand Relief

Whatever happened to friends like Liz,
who curled her legs on a leather settee,
and touched your knee, girl/girl,
as she whispered what the businessmen of Edinburgh
wear beneath their suits –

laughed and hooked her hair back
saying Tuesday, giving some bloke
hand relief, she'd looked up at the ceiling
for the hundredth time that lunch-hour,
and screaming, slammed the other hand down hard
on the panic button; had to stand there
topless in front of the bouncers
and the furious punter, saying
sorry, I'm sorry, it was just a spider . . .

Whatever happens to girls like Liz
fresh out of school, at noon on a Saturday
waiting for her shift at Hotspots
sauna, in a dressing gown
with a pink printed bunny
who follows you to the window
as you look out at the city
and calls you her pal. She says, *you're a real pal*.

Child with Pillar Box and Bin Bags

But it was the shadowed street-side she chose
while Victor Gold the bookies basked
in conquered sunlight, and though
Dalry Road Licensed Grocer gloried and cast
fascinating shadows she chose
the side dark in the shade of tenements;
that corner where Universal Stores' (closed
for modernisation) blank hoarding blocked
her view as if that process were illegal;
she chose to photograph her baby here,
the corner with the pillar box.
In his buggy, which she swung to face her.
She took four steps back, but
the baby in his buggy rolled toward the kerb.
She crossed the ground in no time
it was fearful as Niagara,
she ran to put the brake on, and returned
to lift the camera, a cheap one.
The tenements of Caledonian Place neither
watched nor looked away, they are friendly buildings.
The traffic ground, the buildings shook, the baby breathed
and maybe gurgled at his mother as she
smiled to make him smile in his picture;
which she took on the kerb in the shadowed corner,
beside the post-box, under tenements, before
the bin-bags hot in the sun that shone
on them, on dogs, on people on the other side

the other side of the street to that she'd chosen,
if she'd chosen or thought it possible to choose.

School Reunion

1

We were always the first to get snow
up here in the hills, sagging on roofs
like a shirt tail
        laying on the dreels
rich brown before they built more houses.

It's time. Taxis crunch the gravel
        at the Kestrel Hotel, its fake
coach-lamps shine yellow.

             Come in, we're
                almost
                      all here.

Downstairs, women
who work in banks are dancing, handbags
piled like ashes at their feet.

They raise their arms
in the disco lights, bra straps droop,
those faces turn, eyes, the same
lipstick mouths . . .
        In the Ladies/
           Girls

A glass vase & twist of plastic fuchsia.
    Laughter   Hairspray
      holds   the air
smiles stale
        fag ash   grey
cubicle doors clang; my shoes are wrong
                the tongue
                shocks with blood
                fuck off you

a pin scratches:
      I want McKean
      to shag me – Gemma
          is a bitch whore slag tart
                Our voices
rise and rise, breasts fall
      toward pink-pastel basins,
         as we take out lipsticks, lean
into mirrors   look   our mother's faces
         rise to greet us
         framed in paper rosebuds
           from the opposite wall.

2
The child birls in the frosty playground,
her woolly hat, gloves flying on strings.

The text of a dream: wild earth
                        carpet
emulsion in peach blossom.
                Decree Nisi, two years
        South Australia;
                        we have
                        almost all come back

the D.J. who lived down the lane,

Linda   willowy acrobat
divorce   cartwheels, skirts
Expecting   (again)   cover her face

        a mother's grip
    can't you be more
            ladylike,   women
                                beware
                                gravity.

Lorraine Paton   (she's started
Gillian   she's started
that Michelle   She started and all
            ganging up, the fruity weight of a gang
            swaying slowly, ganging up.
                            You!

                    snot-bag
          Ya: Fat boy, Lezzie
     ya spaz, gowk, snobby get, ya poofter

that Sandra

we knew each other utterly, the spinning bairn

                              ya lying cow she never
               threw herself under a train

The grey clanging metal lavvy doors.

     3
Oh who
                    is that: gliding between darkened tables
                    turquoise and gold strap, tropical blackhair
                    on a bare arm tiny
                    diamond in her slender nose o who
                         in the disco-lights . . .
                    Couldn't I have dared to be
                    Hazel Thompson, the weight of all hair
                    lists her head as though she hears
                    birdsong in Africa
                    through the stamping disco
                    tilts as the diamond
                    tugs toward its black mine

hair grown since we were
seven   secret as marijuana
in her dad's shed
    their council house maroon door.
I'd like to
gather up that black hair
Clarks shoes slapping
down the street straight and grey
as a school skirt, rainwater stains
on harled gables, NO BALL GAMES
to see her in turquoise and gold
give it her in armfuls, Hazel
witchy
sweet as a   wait, *let me*

            chum you . . .

Oh who   would have thought it?

4

When we're older than a mattress
on the dump, and shudder
in the living rooms of daughters
who're 60, who put on lipstick and
kindly lead us out
    to lunch in cold hotels
  that smell of paint, specimen
vases with plastic fuchsias
   and our shoes are wrong, shuffling on the red carpet,
  again we'll enter The Kestrel Hotel's
dim loud dance hall;

as diners turn in the cool light,
mouth open, those appalled young eyes;
we know whose names we will mutter & shout
we are almost all here
as our daughters hush us.

5

The first snow. Taxis turn
onto the high road,
the Wimpey scheme's
familiar streets. Distant lights
flash calmly
on the Forth Bridge, warning aircraft.

The morning after, waking
in your parents' too-small house,
the single bed, & wardrobe
brought from Granny's when she died

Today we'll take a walk
flat shoes, damp stains
on the harled gables;
to the fields; perhaps
a kestrel
hovering still above the road.

Our laughter sealed in taxis, those faces
turn, eyes, same lipstick mouths;
goodbyes   your corner
with the privet hedge whose leaves

like greasy silk you pulled
one by one, under the streetlamp.

In yellow light, the bairn spins

a coloured twist
within us, like a marble.
Close the taxi door and wave
know we are the space
the others ease into
at your old road-end.

The taxi lights recede through the scheme's
dour streets   You watch
from the same door,
then let yourself in.

As if
it's never happened
all that's happened since.

Wee Wifey

I have a demon and her name is
                  WEE WIFEY
I caught her in a demon trap – the household of my skull
I pinched her by her heel throughout her wily transformations
until
      she confessed
                  her name indeed to be WEE WIFEY
and she was out to do me ill.

So I made great gestures like Jehovah: dividing
land from sea, sea from sky,
                  my own self from WEE WIFEY
(*There*, she says, *that's tidy!*)

Now I watch her like a dolly
keep an eye,
         and mourn her:
for she and I are angry/cry
                because we love each other dearly.
It's sad to note
        that without
                WEE WIFEY
I shall live long and lonely as a tossing cork.

Mr and Mrs Scotland Are Dead

On the civic amenity landfill site,
the coup, the dump beyond the cemetery
and the 30-mile-an-hour sign, her stiff
old ladies' bags, open mouthed, spew
postcards sent from small Scots towns
in 1960: Peebles, Largs, the rock-gardens
of Carnoustie, tinted in the dirt.
Mr and Mrs Scotland, here is the hand you were dealt:
fair but cool, showery but nevertheless,
Jean asks kindly; the lovely scenery;
in careful school-room script –
The Beltane Queen was crowned today.
But Mr and Mrs Scotland are dead.

Couldn't he have burned them? Released
in a grey curl of smoke
this pattern for a cable knit? Or this:
tossed between a toppled fridge
and sweet-stinking anorak: *Dictionary for Mothers*
M:– Milk, *the woman who worries . . . ;*
And here, Mr Scotland's John Bull Puncture Repair Kit;
those days when he knew intimately
the thin roads of his country, hedgerows
hanged with small black brambles' hearts;
and here, for God's sake, his last few joiners' tools,
SCOTLAND, SCOTLAND, stamped on their tired handles.

Do we take them? Before the bulldozer comes
to make more room, to shove aside
his shaving brush, her button tin.
Do we save this toolbox, these old-fashioned views
addressed, after all, to Mr and Mrs Scotland?
Should we reach and take them? And then?
Forget them, till that person enters
our silent house, begins to open
to the light our kitchen drawers,
and performs for us this perfunctory rite:
the sweeping up, the turning out.

Arraheids

See thon raws o flint arraheids
in oor gret museums o antiquities
awful grand in Embro –
Dae'ye near'n daur wunner at wur histrie?
Weel then, Bewaur!
The museums of Scotland are wrang.
They urnae arraheids
but a show o grannies' tongues,
the hard tongues o grannies
aa deid an gaun
back to thur peat and burns,
but for thur sherp
chert tongues, that lee
fur generations in the land
like wicked cherms, that lee
aa douce in the glessy cases in the gloom
o oor museums, an
they arenae lettin oan. But if you daur
som aboot an fancy
the vanished hunter, the wise deer runnin on;
wheesht ... an you'll hear them,
fur they cannae keep fae muttering
ye arenae here tae wonder,
whae dae ye think ye ur?

Den of the Old Men

C'mon ye auld buggers, one by one
this first spring day, slowly down
the back braes with your walking sticks
and wee brown dugs, saying: *Aye, lass
a snell wind yet but braw.* Ye
half dozen relics of strong men
sat in kitchen chairs
behind the green gingham curtain
of yer den, where a wee dog grins
on last year's calendar – we hear ye
clacking dominoes the afternoon for pennies.
And if some wee tyke
puts a chuckie through the window
ye stuff yesterday's Courier
in the broken pane, saying
jail's too guid fur them, tellies in cells!
                    We can see your bunnets nod
and jaws move: what're ye up to
now you've your hut built,
now green hame-hammered benches
appear in the parish's secret soft-spots
like old men's spoor?
Is it carties? A tree-hoose?
Or will ye drag up driftwood;
and when she's busy with the bairns
remove your daughters' washing-lines
to lash a raft? Which,

if ye don't all fall out and argue
you can name the *Pride o' Tay* and launch
some bright blue morning on the ebb-tide
and sail away, the lot of yez,
staring straight ahead
               like captains
as you grow tiny
out on the wide Firth, tiny
as you drift past Ballinbriech, Balmurnie, Flisk
with your raincoats and bunnets,
                   wee dugs and sticks.

One of Us

We are come in a stone boat,
a miracle ship that steers itself
round skerries where guillemots
and shags stand still as graves.
Our sealskin cloaks are clasped
by a fist-sized penannular brooch,
our slippers are feathery
gugas' necks: so delicate
we carried them over the wracky shore,
past several rusted tractors. Truth:
this was a poor place, a
ragged land all worn to holes. No one,
nothing, but a distant
Telecom van, a bungalow
tied with fishing floats
for want of flowers.
                That August night
the Perseid shower rained
on moor and lily-loch, on a frightened world –
on us, in a roofless shieling
with all our tat: the
golden horn of righteousness,
the justice harp; what folks expect.
We took swans' shape
to cross the Minch, one last fling
with silly magic – at our first
mainland steps a dormobile

slewed into a passing place; cameras flashed.
So we stayed high, surprised
a forester making aeolian flutes
from plastic tubes,
he shared his pay. 'Avoid
the A9. For God's sake,
get some proper clothes.' We ditched
the cloaks, bought yellow
Pringle sweaters in Spean Bridge,
and house by safe house
arrived in Edinburgh. So far so
tedious: we all hold
minor government jobs, lay plans, and bide our time.

Swallows and Swifts

Twitter of swallows and swifts:
'tickets and visas, visas and tickets' –
winter, and cold rain
clears the milky-way of birdshit
where wires cross the lane.

The Republic of Fife

Higher than the craw-stepped
gables of our institutes – chess-clubs,
fanciers, reels & Strathspeys –
the old kingdom of lum, with crowns agley.

All birds will be citizens: banners
of starlings; Jacobin crows –
also: Sonny Jim Aitken, Special P.C.
whose red face closed in polis cars

utters *terrible, ridiculous*
at his brother and sister citizens
but we're no feart, not of anyone
with a tartan nameplate screwed to his door.

Citizen also: the tall fellow I watched
lash his yurt to the leafy earth,
who lifted his chin
to my greeting, roared AYE !

as in YES! FOREVER! MYSELF!
The very woods where my friend Isabel
once saw a fairy, blue as a gas flame
dancing on trees. All this

close to the motorway
where a citizen has dangled,
maybe with a friend clutching
his/her ankles to spray

PAY NO POLL TAX on a flyover
near to Abernethy, in whose tea rooms
old Scots kings and bishops in mitres
supped wi a lang spoon. Citizens:

our spires and doocoots
institutes and tinkies' benders,
old Scots kings and dancing fairies
give strength to my house

on whose roof we can balance,
carefully stand and see
clear to the far off mountains,
cities, rigs and gardens,

Europe, Africa, the Forth and Tay bridges,
even dare let go, lift our hands
and wave to the waving citizens
of all those other countries.

The Sea-house

In this house
are secret rotting wings,
wrecked timbers; the cupboard
under the stair
glimmers with pearl.

The sea-house
rises from dulse; salt winds
boom in its attics. Here:
my tottering
collections of shells, my ballroom
swirling with fulmars.

Morning brings
laundries of wrack,
a sea-maw's grief-shaped wing. Once
a constellation
of five pink buoys.

This place is a stranger's.
Ewers in each high room
hold a little salt water.
My musical box
is a tinkling crab.

The sea-house is purdah:
cormorants' hooked-out wings
screen every chamber. Inside
the shifting place, the
neither-nor

I knock back and forth
like the tongue of a bell
mournfully tolling
in fog, or lie
as if in a small boat
adrift in an upstairs room.

Rooms

Though I love this travelling life and yearn
like ships docked, I long
for rooms to open with my bare hands,
and there discover the wonderful, say
a ship's prow rearing, and a ladder
of rope thrown down.
Though young, I'm weary:
I'm all rooms at present, all doors
fastened against me;
but once admitted start craving
and swell for a fine, listing ocean-going prow
no man in creation can build me.

At Point of Ness

The golf course shifts
uneasily beside the track
where streetlight melts
to a soft frontier with winter dark.
I cross, then, helpless as a ship,
must let night load me, before
moving on between half-sensed
dry-stane walls; day-birds tucked in some nook.

Tonight, the darkness roars.
Even the fishermen's
Nissen hut seems to breathe
beside its spawn of creels,
a dreadful beaching. I walk on,
toward the shore, where night's
split open, the entire
archipelago set as sink-weight
to the sky. A wind's

caught me now; breath frosts,
and I count, to calm me, the Sound's
lighthouses as they shine and fade
across the surge. Graemsay
beams a long systolic five
to one of dark; Hoy a distant
two: two; scattered buoys
blink where skerries drown, then cut

to sea and stars, then
bloom again, weird lilies
wilt and bloom, till,
heart-scared, I have it
understood:
       never   *ever*
harm – this,
                 you never could

and run – that constant roar,
the track's black vein; toward salt
lit windows, my own door . . .

Skeins o Geese

Skeins o geese write a word
across the sky. A word
struck lik a gong
afore I wis born.
The sky moves like cattle, lowin.

I'm as empty as stane, as fields
ploo'd but not sown, naked
an blin as a stane. Blin
tae the word, blin
tae a' soon but geese ca'ing.

Wire twists lik archaic script
roon a gate. The barbs
sign tae the wind as though
it was deef. The word whustles
ower high for ma senses. Awa.

No lik the past which lies
strewn aroun. Nor sudden death.
No like a lover we'll ken
an connect wi forever.
The hem of its goin drags across the sky.

Whit dae birds write on the dusk?
A word niver spoken or read.
The skeins turn hame,
on the wind's dumb moan, a soun,
maybe human, bereft.

From Jizzen
(1999)

Crossing the Loch

Remember how we rowed toward the cottage
on the sickle-shaped bay,
that one night after the pub
loosed us through its swinging doors
and we pushed across the shingle
till water lipped the sides
as though the loch mouthed 'boat'?

I forget who rowed. Our jokes hushed.
The oars' splash, creak, and the spill
of the loch reached long into the night.
Out in the race I was scared:
the cold shawl of breeze,
and hunched hills; what the water held
of deadheads, ticking nuclear hulls.

Who rowed, and who kept their peace?
Who hauled salt-air and stars
deep into their lungs, were not reassured;
and who first noticed the loch's
phosphorescence, so, like a twittering nest
washed from the rushes, an astonished
small boat of saints, we watched water shine
on our fingers and oars,
the magic dart of our bow wave?

It was surely foolhardy, such a broad loch, a tide,
but we live – and even have children
to women and men we had yet to meet
that night we set out, calling our own
the sky and salt-water, wounded hills
dark-starred by blaeberries, the glimmering anklets
we wore in the shallows
as we shipped oars and jumped,
to draw the boat safe, high at the cottage shore.

The Graduates

If I chose children they'd know
stories of the old country, the place
we never left. I swear

I remember no ship
slipping from the dock,
no cluster of hurt, proud family

waving till they were wee
as china milkmaids
on a mantelpiece,

but we have surely gone,
and must knock
with brass kilted pipers

the doors to the old land;
we emigrants of no farewell
who keep our bit language

in jokes and quotes;
our working knowledge
of coal-pits, fevers, lost

like the silver bangle I lost
at the shows one Saturday,
tried to conceal, denied

but they're not daft.
And my bright, monoglot bairns
will discover, misplaced

among the bookshelves,
proof, rolled in a red tube:
my degrees, a furled sail, my visa.

Forget It

History in a new scheme. I stretch
through hip, ribs, oxter, bursting
the cuff of my school shirt, because
this, Mr Hanning, is me.
'Sir! Sir! Sir!
– he turns, and I claim
just one of these stories,
razed places, important as castles,
as my own. *Mum!*

We done the slums today!
I bawled from the glass
front door she'd long desired.
What for? bangs the oven shut,
Some history's better forgot.
                    So how come
we remember the years
before we were born? Gutters
still pocked with fifties rain,
trams cruised dim
street-lit afternoons; war
at our backs. The black door
of the close wheezed
till you turned the third stair
then resounded like cannon.
A tower of bannisters. Nana
and me toiled past windows

smeared in blackout, condemned
empty stone. The neighbours had flitted
to council-schemes, or disappeared . . .

Who were the disappeared? Whose
the cut-throat
razor on the mantelpiece, what man's
coat hung thick with town gas, coal
in the lobby press?
         And I mind
being stood, washed like a dog
with kettle and one cold tap
in a sink plumbed sheer
from the window
to the back midden
as multistoreys rose
across the goods yard,
and shunters clanked
through nights shared
in the kitchen recess bed.

I dreamed about my sister in America
I doot she's dead. What rural
feyness this? Another sibling
lost in Atlantic cloud,
a hint of sea in the rain –
the married in England,
the drunken and the mad,
a couple of notes postmarked Canada,
then mist: but this is a past

not yet done, else how come
our parents slam shut, deny
like criminals: *I can't remember, cannae
mind*, then turn at bay: *Why?*

Who wants to know? Stories
spoken through the mouths
of closes: who cares
who trudged those worn stairs,
or played in now rubbled back greens?
*What happened about my granddad? Why
did Agnes go? How come
you don't know*

that stories are balm,
ease their own pain, contain
a beginning, a middle –
and ours is a long driech
now-demolished street. *Forget it!*
Forget them that vanished,
voted with their feet,
away for good
or ill through the black door
even before the great clearance came,
turning tenements outside-in,
exposing gas pipes, hearths
in damaged gables, wallpaper
hanging limp and stained
in the shaming rain.

History, Mr Hanning.
The garden shrank for winter,
and mum stirred our spaghetti hoops
not long before she started back
part-time at Debenhams
to save for Christmas,
the odd wee
luxury, our first
foreign
holiday.

Ultrasound

(for Duncan)

I. ULTRASOUND

Oh whistle and I'll come to ye,
my lad, my wee shilpit ghost
summonsed from tomorrow.

Second sight,
a seer's mothy flicker,
an inner sprite:

this is what I see
with eyes closed;
a keek-aboot among secrets.

If Pandora
could have scanned
her dark box,

and kept it locked –
this ghoul's skull, punched eyes
is tiny Hope's,

hauled silver-quick
in a net of sound,
then, for pity's sake, lowered.

II. SOLSTICE

To whom do I talk, an unborn thou,
sleeping in a bone creel.

Look what awaits you:
stars, milk-bottles, frost
on a broken outhouse roof.

Let's close the door,
and rearrange
the dark red curtain.

Can you tell the days are opening,
admit a touch more light,
just a touch more?

III. THAW

When we brought you home in a taxi
through the steel-grey thaw
after the coldest week in memory
– even the river sealed itself –
it was I, hardly breathing,
who came through the passage to our yard
welcoming our simplest things:
a chopping block, the frost-
split lintels; and though it meant a journey
through darkening snow,

arms laden with you in a blanket,
I had to walk to the top of the garden,
to touch, in a complicit
homage of equals, the spiral
trunks of our plum trees, the moss,
the robin's roost in the holly.
Leaning back on the railway wall,
I tried to remember;
but even my footprints were being erased
and the rising stars of Orion
denied what I knew: that as we were
hurled on a trolley through swing doors to theatre
they'd been there, aligned on the ceiling,
    ablaze with concern
for that difficult giving,
before we were two, from my one.

IV. FEBRUARY

To the heap of nappies
carried from the automatic
in a red plastic basket

to the hanging out, my mouth
crowded with pegs;
to the notched prop

hoisting the wash,
a rare flight of swans,
hills still courying snow;

to spring's hint sailing
the westerly, snowdrops
sheltered by rowans –
to the day of St Bride, the first
sweet-wild weeks of your life
I willingly surrender.

V. Bairnsang

Wee toshie man,
       gean tree and rowan
gif ye could staun
yer feet wad lichtsome tread
granite an saun,
but ye cannae yet staun
sae maun courie tae ma airm
an greetna, girna, Gretna Green

Peedie wee lad
       saumon, siller haddie
gin ye could rin
ye'd rin richt easy-strang
ower causey an carse,
but ye cannae yet rin
sae maun jist courie in
and fashna, fashna, Macrahanish Sand

Bonny wee boy
      peeswheep an whaup
gin ye could sing, yer sang

wad be caller
as a lauchin mountain burn
but ye cannae yet sing
sae maun courie tae ma hert
an grieve nat at aa, Ainster an Crail

My ain tottie bairn
      sternie an lift
gin ye could daunce, yer daunce
wad be that o life itsel,
but ye cannae yet daunce
sae maun courie in my erms
and sleep, saftly sleep, Unst and Yell

VI. SEA URCHIN

Between my breast
and cupped hand,
      your head

rests as tenderly
as once I may
      have freighted

water, or drawn
treasure, whole
      from a rockpool

with no premonition
of when next I find one
cast up
      broken.

VII. Prayer

Our baby's heart, on the sixteen-week scan
was a fluttering bird, held in cupped hands.

I thought of St Kevin, hands opened in prayer
and a bird of the hedgerow nesting there,

and how he'd borne it, until the young had flown
— and I prayed: this new heart must outlive my own.

The Tay Moses

What can I fashion
for you but a woven
creel of river-
rashes, a golden
oriole's nest, my gift
wrought from the Firth –

and choose my tide: either
the flow, when, watertight
you'll drift to the uplands –
my favourite hills; held safe
in eddies, where salmon, wisdom
and guts withered in spawn,
rest between moves – that
slither of body as you were born –

or the ebb, when the water
will birl you to snag
on reeds, the river-
pilot leaning over the side:
'Name o God!' and you'll change hands:
tractor-man, grieve, farm-wife
who takes you into her
competent arms

even as I drive, slamming
the car's gears,
spitting gravel on tracks
down between berry-fields,
engine still racing, the door wide
as I run toward her, crying
LEAVE HIM! Please,
it's okay, he's mine.

Bonaly

How did we discover our neat fit?
That critical inch, letting her slip
beneath my right arm, her left
snug on my waist? She had the practised
step of a sword-dance medallist,
and I was sensible, possessed
a Girl Guide uniform
stamped and stamped with badges

and knew how tight to tie
the maroon cotton strip. Ach
it would all go to hell soon enough,
but just that once, on a school pitch
in a Wimpey scheme in Midlothian,
me and Fiona Murray
could beat all comers, pounding
past our shrieking classmates

with our two heads, three legs
like some abomination
the midwife might have smothered
and for what? All for the greater
glory of Bonaly, our House, denoted
by a red sash and named for a loch
somewhere high in the Pentlands –
a place we could scarcely imagine. *Bonaly!*

Flower-sellers, Budapest

In the gardens
of their mild southern crofts, their
end-of-the-line hillside vineyards,
where figs turn blue, and peppers dry
strung from the eaves,
old women move among flowers,
each with a worn knife, a sliver
crooked in the first finger
of her right hand –
each, like her neighbours,
drawing the blade
onto the callus of her thumb,
so flowers, creamy dahlias,
fall into their arms; the stems'
spittle wiped on their pinafores.

Then, when they have enough,
the old women
foregather at the station
to await the slow, busy little train
that will take them to the city,
where families drift between mass
and lunch; and they hunker
at bus depots, termini
scented with chrysanthemums,
to pull from plastic buckets
yellows, spicy russets,

the petally nub of each flower
tight as a bee;
and from their pockets, pink ribbon
strictly for the flowers.

We must buy some,
– though they will soon wither –
from this thin-faced
widow in a headscarf, this mother
perhaps, of married daughters
down at the border –
or *this* old woman, sat
among pigeons and lottery kiosks,
who reaches towards us to proffer
the morning's fresh blooms;
or the woman there who calls 'Flowers!'
in several languages –
one for each invasion:

We must buy some,
because only when the flowers are dispersed
will the old women head for home,
each with her neighbours,
back where they came, with their
empty buckets and thick aprons
on a late morning train.

Song of Sunday

A driech day, and nothing to do
bar watch starlings fluchter
over soup bones
left on a plate on the grass.
All forenoon broth-barley, marrowfat peas
swelled in a kitchen jug,
and I soaked stamps, corners
torn from polite white envelopes
in a saucer till they peeled clear,
neither soggy nor still stuck: 'See,
watch and not tear them, wait at peace.'

There'd aye be women
in the kitchen, brisket
lashed in string, tatties
peeled lovelessly, blinded
pale and drowned. *See if one*
now nicked herself
with a paring knife
and spellbound, the house froze —
only now, hacking back in
through privet and rowan,
toward my father caught
mid stretch and yawn,
my wee sister playing Sindys
with the girl next door,
could I wake them

with something alien
and lovely
as a kiss.

– and we'd be called to eat
what's put in front of us: potatoes, meat
till we could get down, *Please*.
There were African leopards on TV
and *Songs of Praise*. My stamps were dry,
the odd USA, Magyar Poste exotic
among the tuppenny-ha'penny pinks,
the wee lion
rampant in a corner
and after homework I'd have time
to turn to 'Great Britain'
like I'd been shown,
fold and align the edges
with the orderly squares.
Press. 'Bedtime!' *There.*

Hackit

*(after a photograph in the museum of
Sault Ste-Marie, Ontario)*

For every acre cleared, a cairn's raised:
a woman, staggering, stone
after stone in her hands. Desire's

wiped from her eyes,
who once touched to her face
all the linen a bride might need,

her sister closing
till their hands met, sheets
folded and stowed in the hold,

and the gatherings of land –
Arran, Bute, the Heads of Ayr
parted as the ship sailed.

Snow layers fields, and trees blur.
She stares from a door,
fingers splayed, face

hackit
under the lace mutch
brought from her box.

But they'd still recognize
her accent, when steadily
she told about surviving

their first winter:
the flour barrels, empty,
the last herring, small as her hand.

Lochan

(For Jean Johnstone)

When all this is over I mean
to travel north, by the high

drove roads and cart tracks
probably in June,

with the gentle dog-roses
flourishing beside me. I mean

to find among the thousands
scattered in that land

a certain quiet lochan,
where water lilies rise

like small fat moons,
and tied among the reeds,

underneath a rowan,
a white boat waits.

Rhododendrons

They were brought under sail
from a red-tinged east,
carried down gangplanks
in dockers' arms. Innocent
and rare. Their thick leaves
bore a salt-damp gleam,
their blooms a hidden gargle
in their green throats.

Shuddering on trains
to Poolewe, or Arduine,
where the head gardener leaned
across the factor's desk. On a hill
above the sparkling loch
he spoke to his hands,
and terraces were cut,
sites marked, shallow holes dug

before they were turned out.
– Such terribly gentle
work, the grasping of the fat
glazed pots, the fertile
globe of the root-ball
undisturbed, Yunnan
or Himalayan earth
settled with them.

So we step out from their shade
to overlook Loch Melfort
and the bare glens, ready now
to claim this flowering, purple
flame-bright exotica as our own;
a commonplace, native
as language or living memory,
to our slightly acid soil.

Lucky Bag

Tattie scones, St Andra's banes,
a rod-and-crescent Pictish stane,
a field o whaups, organic neeps,
a poke o Brattisani's chips;
a clootie well, computer bits,
an elder o the wee free Kirk;

a golach fi Knoydart,
a shalwar-kemeez;
Dr Simpson's anaesthetics, *zzzzzzzz*,
a gloup, a clachan, a Broxburn bing,
a giro, a demo, Samye Ling;

a ro-ro in the gloaming,
a new-born Kirkcaldy
baby-gro; a Free State, a midden,
a chambered cairn –
yer Scottish lucky-bag, one for each wean;
please form an orderly
                                        rabble.

The Well at the Broch of Gurness

Imagine the sails flying like swans,
women hauling infants
as ox-horns bawled,
and door-bars thudding
home in this socket, where a thrush nests.

And slipping away from the rest
– a girl, crossing flagstones
to the sunken well, where, left hand
on the roof's cool rock,
she steps down out of the world.

Perhaps she's there yet, waiting
till they've done their worst
before she drinks, then barefoot
begins her return toward daylight,
where she'll vanish.

The broch's rubble.
Her homestead's lintels tilt
through mown turf.
But we can follow her, descend
below the bright grasses, the beat of surf

step by hewn step, crouching
till our eyes adjust – before we seek
the same replenishing water,
invisible till reached for,
when reached for, touched.

St Bride's

(For Freya)

So this is women's work: folding
and unfolding, be it linen or a selkie-
skin tucked behind a rock. Consider

the hare in jizzen: her leverets' ears
flat as the mizzen of a ship
entering a bottle. A thread's trick;

adders uncoil into spring. Feathers
of sunlight, glanced from a butterknife
quiver on the ceiling,

and a last sharp twist for the shoulders
delivers my daughter, the placenta
following, like a fist of purple kelp.

The Green Woman

Until we're restored to ourselves
by weaning, the skin jade
only where it's hidden
under jewellery, the areolae still tinged,
– there's a word for women like us.

It's suggestive of the lush
ditch, or even an ordeal,
– as though we'd risen,
tied to a ducking-stool,
gasping, weed-smeared, proven.

Bolus

So little of the world is bequeathed
through us, our gifts
instead, are passed among the living
– like words, or the bolus
of chewed bread
a woman presses with her tongue
into the gorgeous open mouth of her infant.

On the Design Chosen for the
New Scottish Parliament Building
by Architect Enric Miralles

An upturned boat
      – a watershed.

Meadowsweet

*Tradition suggests that certain of the Gaelic
women poets were buried face down.*

So they buried her, and turned home,
a drab psalm hanging
about them like haar,

not knowing the liquid
trickling from her lips
would seek its way down,

and that caught in her slowly
unravelling plait of grey hair
were summer seeds:

meadowsweet, bastard balm,
tokens of honesty, already
beginning their crawl

toward light, so showing her,
when the time came,
how to dig herself out –

to surface and greet them,
mouth young, and full again
of dirt, and spit, and poetry

From THE TREE HOUSE
(2004)

The Wishing Tree

I stand neither in the wilderness
nor fairyland

but in the fold
of a green hill

the tilt from one parish
into another.

To look at me
through a smirr of rain

is to taste the iron
in your own blood

because I hoard
the common currency

of longing: each wish
each secret assignation.

My limbs lift, scabbed
with greenish coins

I draw into my slow wood
fleur-de-lys, the enthroned Britannia.

Behind me, the land
reaches towards the Atlantic.

And though I'm poisoned
choking on the small change

of human hope,
daily beaten into me

look: I am still alive —
in fact, in bud.

Frogs

But for her green
palpitating throat, they lay
inert as a stone, the male
fastened like a package
to her back. They became,

as you looked, almost
beautiful, her back
mottled to leafy brown,
his marked with two stripes,
pale as over-wintered grass.

When he bucked, once,
neither so much as blinked;
their oval, gold-lined eyes
held to some bog-dull
imperative. The car

that would smear them
into one – belly
to belly, tongue thrust
utterly into soft brain –
approached and pressed on

Oh how we press on –
the car and passengers, the slow
creatures of this earth,
the woman by the verge
with her hands cupped

Alder

Are you weary, alder tree,
in this, the age of rain?

From your branches
droop clots of lichen

like fairy lungs. All week,
squalls, tattered mists:

alder, who unfolded
before the receding glaciers

first one leaf then another,
won't you teach me

a way to live
on this damp ambiguous earth?

The rain showers
release from you a broken tune

but when the sun blinks, as it must,
how you'll sparkle –

like a fountain in a wood
of untold fountains.

The Cave of the Fish

It winds through sage,
cypresses, rock rose –
the drove road long

shared by goatherds
and fisherfolk. At noon
they'd retreat to a high cave,

seclude their wares
deep in its shade,
talk there, or doze.

Though some of them
had a whiff of the beast,
others a hint of brine,

the path below led home
for both, neither
more true nor more right.

Today I sit at the cave's
cool mouth, halfway
through my life.

Before the Wind

If I'm to happen upon the hill
where cherries grow wild
it better be soon, or the yellow-
eyed birds will come squabbling,

claiming the fruit for their own.
Wild means stones barely
clothed in flesh, but that's rich
coming from me. A mouth

contains a cherry, a cherry
a stone, a stone
the flowering branch
I must find before the wind

scatters all trace of its blossom,
and the fruit comes, and yellow-eyed birds.

Speirin

Binna feart, hinny,
yin day we'll gang thegither
tae thae stourie
blaebellwids,
and loss wirsels –

see, I'd rather
whummel a single oor
intae the blae o thae wee flo'ers
than live fur a' eternity
in some cauld hivvin.

Wheest, nou, till I spier o ye
will ye haud wi me?

Landfall

When we walk at the coast
and notice, above the sea,
a single ragged swallow
veering towards the earth-
and blossom-scented breeze,
can we allow ourselves to fail

The Bower

Neither born nor gifted
crafted nor bequeathed
this forest dwelling's little
but a warp or tease

in the pliant light
trees soften and confine.
Though it's nothing
but an attitude of mind

mere breath rising in staves,
the winds assail
its right to exist, this anchorage
or musical box, veiled

and listing deep
in the entailed estate,
sure only of its need
to annunciate.

But when song,
cast from such frail enclaves
meets the forest's edge,
it returns in waves

Swallows

I wish my whole battened
heart were a property
like this, with swallows
in every room – so at ease

they twitter and preen
from the picture frames
like an audience in the gods
before an opera

and in the mornings
wheel above my bed
in a mockery of pity
before winging it

up the stairwell
to stream out into light

The Blue Boat

How late the daylight edges
toward the northern night
as though journeying
in a blue boat, gilded in mussel shell

with, slung from its mast, a lantern
like our old idea of the soul

Gloaming

We are flying, this summer's night, toward a brink, a wire-thin
rim of light. It swells as we descend, then illuminates the land
enough to let us name, by hill or river mouth, each township below.
This is the North, where people, the world perhaps likes to imagine,
hold a fish in one hand, in the other a candle.
I could settle for that. The plane shudders, then rolls to a standstill
at the far end of the runway. It's not day, this light we've entered,
but day is present at the negotiation. The sky's the still
pale grey of a heron, attending the tide-pools of the shore.

The Glass-hulled Boat

First come the jellyfish:
mauve-fringed, luminous bowls
like lost internal organs,
pulsing and slow.

Then in the green gloom
swaying sideways and back
like half-forgotten ancestors
– columns of bladderwrack.

It's as though we're stalled in a taxi
in an ill-lit, odd
little town, at closing time,
when everyone's maudlin

and really, ought just to *go
home*, you sorry inclining
pillars of wrack, you lone,
vaguely uterine jellyfish

– whom I almost envy:
spun out, when our engines churn,
on some sudden new trajectory,
fuddled, but unperturbed.

White-sided Dolphins

When there was no doubt,
no mistaking for water-glint
their dorsal fins'
urgent cut and dive

we grabbed cameras, threw ourselves
flat on the fore-deck. Then,
just for a short time
we travelled as one

loose formation: the muscular
wingers, mothers-with-young,
old scarred outriders
all breached alongside,

took it in turn
to swoon up through our pressure-wave,
careen and appraise us
with a speculative eye

till they'd seen enough,
when true to their own
inner oceanic maps, the animals
veered off from us, north by northwest.

Basking Shark

When I came to the cliff-edge
and lay down, all beneath
was space, then green-
tinted sea, so clear
it revealed, level below level,
not void, but a living creature.

Behind me peat moor
careered inland. I gripped
sweet rock – but it was only
resting, berthed as though
drawn by the cliff's
peculiar backwash,

precisely that its ore-
heavy body and head –
the tail fin measuring back,
forth, like a haunted door –
could come to sense the absolute
limits of its realm.

While it hung, steady
as an anvil but for the fins'
corrective rippling – dull,
dark and buoyed like a heart
that goes on living
through a long grief

what could one do but watch?
The sea heaved; fulmars
slid by on static wings;
the shark – not ready yet
to re-enter the ocean
travel there, peaceable and dumb –

waited, and was watched;
till it all became
unbearable, whereupon the wind
in its mercy breathed again
and far below the surface
glittered, and broke up.

The Whale-watcher

And when at last the road
gives out, I'll walk –
harsh grass, sea-maws,
lichen-crusted bedrock –

and hole up the cold
summer in some battered
caravan, quartering
the brittle waves

till my eyes evaporate
and I'm willing again
to deal myself in:
having watched them

breach, breathe, and dive
far out in the glare,
like stitches sewn in a rent
almost beyond repair.

Selchs

Daur we, ma jo,
dae lik thae selchs, sae
inglamourt bi the saumon-rin

thae dinnae tak wit
til thur somewhaur wanchancy –
caller-watter, taintit wi peat?

Hame

(efter Hölderlin)

Wha's tae ken
if whiles Ah dauner
yur back-braes, O Yird
and pu wild berries
tae slocken ma luve fur ye
– here whaur jags o roses
and gean-trees
pit oot thur sweet air,
aside the birks, at noon,

when, in the yella glebe
grouin corn reeshles,
and the ickers nod, like at hairst,
– but nou, ablo the aiks' lift,
whaur ah wunner an spier
heivenward, yonner
weel-kent bell jows
gowden notes,
at the oor the birds wauken
ance mair. An a's weel.

The Buddleia

When I pause to consider
a god, or creation unfolding
in front of my eyes –
is this my lot? Always
brought back to the same
grove of statues in ill-
fitting clothes: my suddenly
elderly parents, their broken-down
Hoover; or my quarrelling kids?

Come evening, it's almost too late
to walk in the garden, and try,
once again, to retire the masculine
God of my youth
by evoking instead the divine
in the lupins, or foxgloves, or self-
seeded buddleia,
whose heavy horns flush as they
open to flower, and draw
these bumbling, well-meaning bees
which remind me again,
of my father . . . whom, Christ,
I've forgotten to call.

Pipistrelles

In the centre of the sheep-field
a stand of Douglas firs
hold between them, tenderly,
a tall enclosure like a vase.

How could we have missed it
before today – never have seen
this clear, translucent vessel
tinted like citrine?

What we noticed were pipistrelles:
cinder-like, friable, flickering
the place hained by trees
till the air seemed to quicken

and the bats were a single
edgy intelligence, testing their idea
for a new form
which unfolded and cohered

before our eyes. The world's
mind is such interstices;
cells charging with light of day –
is that what they were telling us?

But they vanished, suddenly,
before we'd understood,
and the trees grew in a circle,
elegant and mute.

Daisies

We are flowers of the common
sward, that much we understand.
Of everything else
we're innocent. No Creator
laid down such terms
for our pleasant lives,
– it's just our nature,
were we not so,
we wouldn't be daisies, closing
our lashes at the first
suggestion of Venus. By then,
we're near exhausted. Evening
means sleep, and surely it's better
to renew ourselves than die
of all that openness?
But die we will, innocent
or no, of how night
spills above our garden,
twins glittering there
for each of us; die
never knowing what we miss.

Hoard

What kind of figure did he cut
huddled in the dusk, gut wound
packed with sphagnum,
as he sank into the bog
his offering of weaponry,
blades courteously broken,
his killed cherished swords?

Moult

At a certain time of year
come floating shorewards
innumerable seabirds'
primaries and coverts.

Though they're dead things
washed up on the sand
each carries a part
– a black tip, say, to the vane –

of the pattern the outstretched
wing displays. What
can one frayed feather
tell of that design,

or the covenant they undertake,
wind and kittiwake?

The Tree House

Hands on a low limb, I braced,
swung my feet loose, hoisted higher,
heard the town clock toll, a car
breenge home from a club
as I stooped inside. Here

I was unseeable. A bletted fruit
hung through tangled branches
just out of reach. Over house roofs:
sullen hills, the firth drained
down to sandbanks: the *Reckit Lady*, the *Shair as Daith*.

I lay to sleep,
beside me neither man
nor child, but a lichened branch
wound through the wooden chamber,
pulling it close; a complicity

like our own, when arm in arm
on the city street, we bemoan
our families, our difficult
chthonic anchorage
in the apple-sweetened earth,

without whom we might have lived
the long ebb of our mid-decades
alone in sheds and attic rooms,

awake in the moonlit souterrains
of our own minds; without whom

we might have lived
a hundred other lives,
like taxis strangers hail and hire,
that turn abruptly on the gleaming setts
and head for elsewhere.

Suppose just for the hell of it
we flagged one – what direction would we give?
Would we still be driven here,
our small-town Ithacas, our settlements
hitched tight beside the river

where we're best played out
in gardens of dockens
and lady's mantle, kids' bikes
stranded on the grass;
where we've knocked together

of planks and packing chests
a dwelling of sorts; a gall
we've asked the tree to carry
of its own dead, and every spring
to drape in leaf and blossom, like a pall.

The Cupboard

As for this muckle
wooden cupboard carted hither
years ago, from some disused
branch-line station, the other
side of the hill, that takes up
more room than the rest of us
put together, like a dour
homesick whale, or mute sarcophagus –

why is it at *my* place?
And how did it sidle
through the racked,
too-narrow door, to hunker
below these sagging rafters,
no doubt for evermore?

The Creel

The world began with a woman,
shawl-happed, stooped under a creel,
whose slow step you recognize
from troubled dreams. You feel

obliged to help bear her burden
from hill or kelp-strewn shore,
but she passes by unseeing
thirled to her private chore.

It's not sea birds or peat she's carrying,
not fleece, nor the herring bright
but her fear that if ever she put it down
the world would go out like a light.

The Brooch

All I have is small enough
to be held in one hand –
an agate brooch. It's pierced

like an implement or tool,
perhaps a loom weight.
The agates are brindled,

grey, like carded wool,
or the rings inside a cup, drained,
set to be washed on a table.

Of the woman who pinned it
to her plain coat, only this remains:
her gift, my heirloom, stones.

The Dipper

It was winter, near freezing,
I'd walked through a forest of firs
when I saw issue out of the waterfall
a solitary bird.

It lit on a damp rock,
and, as water swept stupidly on,
wrung from its own throat
supple, undammable song.

It isn't mine to give.
I can't coax this bird to my hand
that knows the depth of the river
yet sings of it on land.

From THE OVERHAUL
(2012)

The Beach

Now this big westerly's
blown itself out,
let's drive to the storm beach.

A few brave souls
will be there already,
eyeing the driftwood,

the heaps of frayed
blue polyprop rope,
cut loose, thrown back at us –

What a species –
still working the same
curved bay, all of us

hoping for the marvellous,
all hankering for a changed life.

The Dash

Every mid-February
those first days arrive
when the sun rises
higher than the Black
Hill at last. Brightness
and a crazy breeze
course from the same airt −
turned clods gleam, the trees'
topmost branches bend
shivering downwind.
They chase, this lithe pair
out of the far south
west, and though scalding
to our wintered eyes
look, we cry, *it's here*

Ospreys

You'll be wondering why you bothered: beating
up from Senegal, just to hit a teuchit storm –
late March blizzards and raw winds – before the tilt

across the A9, to arrive, mere
hours apart, at the self-same riverside

Scots pine, and possess again the sticks and fishbones
of last year's nest: still here, pretty much
like the rest of us – gale-battered, winter-worn,
       half toppled away . . .

So redd up your cradle, on the tree-top,
claim your teind from the shining
estates of the firth, or the trout-stocked loch.
What do you care? Either way,
there'll be a few glad whispers round town today:
that's them, baith o' them, they're in.

Springs

Full March moon and gale-force easters, the pair of them
sucking and shoving the river
back into its closet in the hills, or trying to. Naturally

the dykes failed, the town's last fishing boat
raved at the pier-head, then went down; diesel-
corrupted water cascaded into front-yards, coal-holes, garages,

and *there's naethin ye can dae*,
said the old boys, the sages, which may be true; but river –
what have you left us? Evidence of an inner life, secrets
of your estuarine soul hawked halfway

up Shore Street, up East and Mid Shore, and arrayed
in swags all through the swing-park: plastic trash and broken reeds,
driftwood, bust TVs . . .
               and a salmon,
dead, flung beneath the see-saw, the crows are onto at once.

May

Again the wild blossom
powering down at dusk, the gean trees
a lather at the hillfoot
              and a blackbird, telling us
what he thinks to it, telling us
              what he thinks . . .
How can we bear it? A fire-streaked sky, a firth
decked in gold, the grey clouds passing
like peasant-folk
              lured away by a prophecy.
                    What can we say
the blackbird's failed
to iterate already? Night calls:
the windows of next-door's glass house
crimson, then go mute

.

Excavation & Recovery

Then specialists arrived, in hi-viz jackets and hardhats
who floundered out every low tide
to the log-boat, lodged
in the mud since the Bronze Age. Eventually

it was floated to the slipway, swung high
in front of our eyes: black, dripping, aboriginal
– an axe-hewn hollowed-out oak
        sent to the city on a truck.

What were you to them, river, who hollered
'Shipping water!' or 'Ca' canny lads!' in some now
long-forgotten tongue?

an estuary with a discharge of 160 cubic metres of water per second
as per the experts' report?
or Tay/Toi/Taum   – a goddess;
            the Flowing(?), the Silent One(?).

Fragment 1

Roe deer,
    breaking from a thicket

bounding over briars
    between darkening trees

you don't even glance
    at the cause of your doubt

so how can you tell
    what form I take?

What form I take
    I scarcely know myself

adrift in a wood
    in wintertime at dusk

always a deer
    breaking from a thicket

for a while now
    this is how it's been

.

The Study

Moon,

      what do you mean,
entering my study
like a curiosity shop,
stroking in mild concern

the telescope mounted
on its tripod, the books,
the attic stair? You
who rise by night, who draw

the inescapable world
closer, a touch,
to your gaze – why
query me? What's mine

is yours; but you've no more
need of those implements
than a deer has,
browsing in a glade.

Moon, your work-
worn face bright
outside unnerves me.
Please, be on your way.

Hawk and Shadow

I watched a hawk
glide low across the hill,
her own dark shape
in her talons like a kill.

She tilted her wings,
fell into the air —
the shadow coursed on
without her, like a hare.

Being out of sorts
with my so-called soul,
part unhooked hawk,
part shadow on parole,

I played fast and loose:
keeping one in sight
while forsaking the other.
The hawk gained height:

her mate on the ground
began to fade,
till hill and sky were empty,
and I was afraid.

The Stags

This is the multitude, the beasts
you wanted to show me, drawing me
upstream, all morning up through wind-
scoured heather to the hillcrest.
Below us, in the next glen, is the grave
calm brotherhood, descended
out of winter, out of hunger, kneeling
like the signatories of a covenant;
their weighty, antique-polished antlers
rising above the vegetation
like masts in a harbour, or city spires.
We lie close together, and though the wind
whips away our man-and-woman smell, every
stag-face seems to look toward us, toward,
but not to us: we're held, and hold them,
in civil regard. I suspect you'd
hoped to impress me, to lift to my sight
our shared country, lead me deeper
into what you know, but loath
to cause fear you're already moving
quietly away, sure I'll go with you,
as I would now, almost anywhere.

A Raised Beach

– of course, that's what –
a plain of stones, perfectly
smooth and still
showing the same slight
ridges and troughs
as thousands of years ago
when the sea left.
– It *is* a sea – even grey
stones one can
walk across: not a
solitary flower, nor a single
blade of grass –
          I know this place
– all with one face
accepting of the sun
the other . . . Moon,
why have you turned to me
your dark side, why am I
examining these stones?
Our friendship lapsed.
– And sea, dear mother,
retreating with long stealth
though I lie awake –
Ah, you're a grown-up now
I've sung to you
quite long enough.

Swifts

When we first emerged, we assumed
what we'd entered
was the world,
and we its only creatures.

Soon, we could fly; soon
we'd mastered its grey gloom,
could steal a single
waterdrop

even as it fell.
Now you who hesitate,
fearful of the tomb-smell,

fearful of shades,
look up – higher!
How deft we are,

how communicative, our
scorch-brown wings almost
translucent against the blue.

Deserts, moonlit oceans, heat
climbing from a thousand coastal cities
are as nothing now,

say our terse screams.
The cave-dark we were born in
calls us back.

The Spider

When I appear to you
by dark, descended
not from heaven, but the lowest
branch of the walnut tree
bearing no annunciation,
suspended like a slub
in the air's weave
and you shriek, you shriek
so prettily, I'm reminded
of the birds – don't birds also
cultivate elaborate beauty, devour
what catches their eye?
Hence my night shift,
my sulphur-and-black-striped
jacket – *poison* – a lie
to cloak me while, exposed,
I squeeze from my own gut
the one material.
　　　　　Who tore the night?
Who caused this rupture?
You, staring in horror
– had you never considered
how the world sustains?
The ants by day
clearing, clearing,
the spiders mending endlessly –

The Gather

The minute the men
ducked through the bothy door
they switched to English.
Even among themselves
they spoke English now,
out of courtesy,
and set about breakfast:
bread, bacon and sweet tea.
And are we enjoying
this weather, and whose
boat brought us, and what
part of the country – exactly –
would we be from ourselves?

– The tenant, ruddy-faced;
a strong bashful youngster,
and two old enough
to be their uncles,
who, planted at the wooden table
seemed happy for a bit crack:
– one with a horse-long,
marvellous weather
and nicotine-scored face
under a felt fedora,
whose every sentence
was a slow sea-wave
raking unhurriedly back

through the rounded
grey stones
at the landing place
where their boat was tied.

Beyond the bothy
– mended since the last gales –
the sea eased west
for miles toward the parishes,
hazy now,
the men had left early.
A sea settled for the meanwhile,
Aye, for the meanwhile!
Then, knocking their tea back,
they were out
round the gable end,
checking the sheep fanks, ready.

High on the island,
uninhabited these days, sheep
grazed oblivious,
till the dogs – the keenest
a sly, heavy-dugged bitch –
came slinking behind them.
Then men appeared, and that
backwash voice: *will you move
you baa-stards!*
Bleating in dismay
the animals zig-zagged down

the vertiginous hill
to spill onto the shore
where they ran, panicked,
and crammed into the fank:
heavy-fleeced mothers
and bewildered lambs,
from whom a truth,
(they now realized)
had been withheld.

'*Ewe-lamb*', '*tup-lamb*',
each animal was seized,
its tail, severed with one snip,
shrugged through the air
to land in a red plastic pail;
each young tup,
upturned, took two men –
doubled over, heads together,
till the lamb's testicles
likewise thumped softly
into the tub, while we joked:
'Oh, will they no' mak a guid soup?'
No – we will deep-fry them,
like they do in Glaa-sgow
with the Maa-rs bars!
Then thrust, one by one
to the next pen, the lambs
huddled in a corner,
and with blood dribbling
down their sturdy

little thighs, they jumped
very lightly, as though in joy.

Summer was passing:
just above the waves,
guillemots whirred toward
their cliff-ledge nests,
but they carried nothing;
few young, this year –
Aye, the birds –
not so many now . . .
and the men stood, considering.
Then it was the ewes:
each in turn, a man's thumb
crossways in her mouth
was tilted upside down
like a small sofa, and clipped
till she stepped out trig
and her fleece
cast over the side:
Fit only to be burned! –
No market nowadays –

All the hot Saturday
the men kept to their work
– a modest living –
pausing every so often
to roll cigarettes, or tilt
plastic bottles of cola
to their parched mouths,

as their denims and tee-shirts
turned slowly rigid
with sweat and wool-grease
and the tide began to lift
fronds of dark weed
as though seeking
something mislaid,
and from the cliffs,
through the constant bleating
came the wild birds'
faint, strangulated cries.

When, late in the day
they were done, the sheep
began to pick their way
up to their familiar pastures –
first the old ewes,
who understood
– if anything – that they,
who take but a small share,
are a living, whom
now and then
a fate visits, like a storm.

But though the sky
was still blue with
teased out clouds,
and the sea brimmed and
lapped at the shore rocks gently,
and they could have rested,

the men wanted away
before the wind rose,
before – they laughed –
the taverns close!
And I run out of tob-aacco!
Before – though they didn't
actually say this – the Sabbath,
so they loaded their boat
– a RIB with a hefty outboard –
and hauled the dogs in.
At first they chugged out
slow and old-fashioned,
like a scene in a documentary,

but suddenly with an arched,
overblown plume
of salt spray
they roared off at top speed,
throwing us a grand wave.

Roses

for M D

This is the moment the roses
cascade over backstreet walls,
throng the public parks –
their cream or scrunched pinks

unfolding now to demonstrate
unacknowledged thought.
The world is ours too! they brave,
careless of tomorrow

and wholly without leadership
for who'd mount a soap-box
on the rose-behalf?

*'I haggle for my little
portion of happiness,'*
says each flower, equal, in the scented mass.

The Overhaul

Look – it's the *Lively*,
hauled out above the tideline
up on a trailer with two
flat tyres. What –

14 foot? Clinker-built
and chained by the stern
to a pile of granite blocks,
but with the bow

still pointed westward
down the long voe,
down toward the ocean,
where the business is.

Inland from the shore
a road runs, for the crofts
scattered on the hill
where washing flaps,

and the school bus calls
and once a week or so
the mobile library;
but see how this

duck-egg green keel's
all salt-weathered,
how the stem, taller
– like a film star –

than you'd imagine,
is raked to hold steady
if a swell picks up
and everyone gets scared . . .

No, it can't be easy,
when the only spray to touch
your boards all summer
is flowers of scentless mayweed;

when little wavelets leap
less than a stone's throw
with your good name
written all over them –

but hey, *Lively*,
it's a time-of-life thing,
it's a waiting game –
patience, patience.

Halfling

Bird on the cliff-top,
the angle of your back
a master-stroke:
why should kittiwakes

plunge at your head
with white shrills?
You're only just falling
from your parents' care,

they've dared slope off
together, to quarter
the island's only glen
leaving you sunlit, burnished,

glaring out to sea
like one bewildered.
Some day soon you'll
topple to the winds

and be gone, a gangrel,
obliged to wander
island to mountain,
taking your chances —

till you moult at last
to an adult's mantle
and settle some scant
estate of your own. Already

the gulls shriek *Eagle!*
Eagle!—they know
more than you
what you'll become.

An Avowal

Bluebell at the wayside
nodding your assent
to summer, and summer's end;
nodding, on your slender stem

your undemurring *yes*
to the small role life
offers you – a few weeks
seasoning the hill-foot grasses

with shakes of blue . . .
You accept, and acquiesce
thereby, to any wind,
though the winds tease:

'Flower,' they ask –
'd'you want to be noticed?'
Yes, yes, noticed!
'Or rather left alone?' *Yes,*

left perfectly alone! 'Flower,'
they whisper, 'd'you love
the breeze that wantons
the whole earth round

breathing its sweet proposals,
but does not love you?'
– then laugh when your blue
head nods: *I do. I do.*

The Galilean Moons

for Nat Jansz

Low in the south sky shines
the stern white lamp
of planet Jupiter. A man
on the radio said
it's uncommonly close;
sequestered in the telescope lens
it's like a compere, spotlit,
driving its borrowed light
out to all sides equally.
While set in a row in the dark
beyond its blaze,
like seed-pearls,
or coy new talents
awaiting their call onstage –
are what must be, surely,
the Galilean moons.

In another room,
my children lie asleep, turning
as Earth turns, growing
into their own lives, leaving me
a short time to watch, eye
to the eye-piece,
how a truth unfolds –

how the moonlets glide
out of their chance alignment,
each again to describe
around its shared host
its own unalterable course.

Tell me, Galileo, is this
what we're working for?
The knowing that in just
one Jovian year
the children will be gone
uncommonly far, their bodies
aglow, grown, talented –
mere bright voice-motes
calling from the opposite
side of the world.
What else would we want
our long-sighted instruments
to assure us of? I'd like
to watch for hours, see
what you old astronomers
apprehended for the first time,
bowing to the inevitable . . .

but it's late. Already
the next day
plucks at my elbow
like a wakeful infant,
next-door's dog barks,
and a cloud arrives,
appearing out of nothing.

The Bridge

Mind thon bridge? The wynds
that spawned us? Those hemmed in,
ramshackle tenements
taller, it seemed, every year . . .

Caller herrin'! Ony rags! On the mountain
stands a lady . . .
What a racket! Coal smoke,
midden-reek . . . filthy,

needless to mention, our two
old hives, heaped high
either side of the river,
crammed with the living, with the dead-beat

and joined by that sandstone ligature . . .
Did you ever notice
how walking out over the water
made us more human:

men became gracious,
women unfolded
their arms from their breasts –
and where else could children,

beggars, any one of us,
pause and look up at the sky!
And that river! Forever
bearing its breeze to the sea,

like a rustic bride, scented
now with blossom,
now with pine sap,
– But what was the sea to us, then?

What was a mountain?
Yes; us. Me and you. *That* bridge,
long ago demolished
where we first met.

Tae the Fates

eftir Hölderlin

Gie me, ye Po'ers, jist ane simmer mair
an ane maumie autumn,
that ma hairt, ripe wi sweet sang,
's no sae swier for tae dee. A sowl

denied in life its heevinly richt
wil waunner Orcus disjaiskit;
but gin ah could mak whit's halie
an maist dear tae me – ane perfect poem

I'll welcome the cauld, the quate mirk!
For though I maun lee' ma lyre
an gang doon wantin sang, Ah'd hae lived,
aince, lik the gods; and aince is eneuch.

Moon

Last night, when the moon
slipped into my attic-room
disguised as an oblong of light,
I sensed she'd come to commiserate.

It was August. She travelled
with a small valise
of darkness, and the first few stars
returning to the northern sky,

and my room, it seemed,
had missed her. She pretended
an interest in the bookcase
while other objects

stirred, as in a rockpool,
with unexpected life:
strings of beads in their green bowl gleamed,
the paper-crowded desk;

the books, too, appeared inclined
to open and confess.
Being sure the moon
harboured some intention,

I waited; watched for an age
her cool gaze shift
first toward a flower sketch
pinned on the far wall

then glide to recline
along the pinewood floor
before I'd had enough. *Moon,*
I said, *we're both scarred now.*

Are they quite beyond you,
the simple words of love? Say them.
You are not my mother;
with my mother, I waited unto death.

Glamourie

When I found I'd lost you –
not beside me, nor ahead,
nor right nor left not
your green jacket moving

between the trees anywhere –
I waited a long while
before wandering on. No wren
jinked in the undergrowth,

not a twig snapped.
It was hardly the Wildwood –
just some auld fairmer's
shelter belt – but red haws

reached out to me,
and between fallen leaves
pretty white flowers bloomed
late into their year. I tried

calling out, or think
I did, but your name
shrivelled on my tongue,
so instead I strolled on

through the wood's good
offices, and duly fell
to wondering if I hadn't
simply made it all up. You,

I mean, everything,
my entire life. Either way,
nothing now could touch me
bar my hosts, who appeared

as diffuse golden light,
as tiny spiders
examining my hair . . .
What gratitude I felt then –

I might be gone for ages,
maybe seven years! –
and such sudden joie de vivre
that when a ditch gaped

right there instantly in front of me
I jumped it, blithe as a girl –
ach, I jumped clear over it,
without even pausing to think.

The Whales

If I could stand the pressures,
if I could make myself strong,

I'd dive far under the ocean,
away from these merfolk

— especially the mermen, moaning
and wringing out their beards.

I'd discover a cave
green and ventricular

and there, with tremendous patience,
I'd teach myself to listen:

what the whale-fish hear
answering through the vastnesses

I'd hear too. But oh my love,
tell me you'd swim by,

tell me you'd look out for me,
down there it's impossible to breathe —

Hauf o' Life

eftir Hölderlin

Bien wi yella pears, fu
o wild roses, the braes
fa intil the loch;
ye mensefu' swans,
drunk wi kisses
dook yir heids
i' the douce, the hailie watter.

But whaur when winter's wi us
will ah fin flo'ers?
Whaur the shadda
an sunlicht o the yird?
Dumbfounert, the wa's staun.
The cauld blast
claitters the wethervanes.

Even the Raven

The grey storm passes
a storm the sea wakes from
then soon forgets . . .

surf plumes at the rocks –
wave after wave, each
drawing its own long fetch

– and the hills across the firth –
golden, as the cloud lifts – yes
it's here, everything

you wanted, everything
you insisted on –

Even the raven,
his old crocked voice

asks you what you're waiting for

Materials

for C.M.

See when it all unravels – the entire project
reduced to threads of moss fleeing a nor'wester;
d'you ever imagine chasing just one strand, letting it lead you
to an unsung cleft in a rock, a place you could take to,
dig yourself in – but what are the chances of that?
                                                    Of the birds,

few remain all winter; half a dozen waders
mediate between sea and shore, that space confirmed
– don't laugh – by your own work. Waves boom, off-white
spume-souls twirl out of geos, and look,

blown about the headland: scraps of nylon fishing net. Gannets
– did you know? – pluck such rubbish from the waves, then hie awa'
to colonies so raucous and thief-ridden, each nest
winds up swagged to the next . . . Then they're flown, and the cliff's left
wearing naught but a shoddy, bird-knitted vest.

And look at us! Out all day and damn all to show for it.
Bird-bones, rope-scraps, a cursory sketch – but a bit o' bruck's
all we need to get us started, all we'll leave behind us when we're gone.

From THE BONNIEST COMPANIE
(2015)

The Shrew

Take me to the river, but not right now,
not in this cauld blast, this easterly
striding up from the sea
        like a bitter shepherd —

and as for you, you Arctic-hatched, comfy-looking geese
        occupying our fields,
you needn't head back north anytime soon —

snow on the mountains, frozen ploughed clods —
weeks of this now, enough's enough

        — but when my hour comes,
let me go like the shrew
right here on the path: spindrift on her midget fur,
        caught mid-thought, mid-dash

Glacial

A thousand-foot slog, then a cairn of old stones –
hand-shifted labour,
and much the same river, shining
                      way below
as the Romans came, saw,
         and soon thought the better of.

Too many mountains, too many
                   wanchancy tribes
whose habits we wouldn't much care for
(but could probably match),
too much grim north, too much faraway snow.

Let's bide here a moment, catching our breath
and inhaling the sweet scent of whatever
                whin-bush is flowering today

and see for miles, all the way hence
to the lynx's return, the re-established wolf's.

Merle

Thon blackbird in the briar
        by the outfield dyke
doesn't know he's born
        doesn't know he's praise and part
of this Sabbath forenoon
        north-Atlantic style.
From his yellow beak his song descends
        to the year's first celandines;
his throat patters. With a yellow claw
he scarts his left lug

Soon the haar will burn off
        revealing the Rum Cuillin
happed in March snow, and the waters of the Minch
        but for now the blackie's
the centre of the world's eye
        – till there! He's flown.

Thon Stane

Thon earthfast boulder by the bothy door,
taller than a man and
                thrice as broad and
older than everyone put together –

stood there in his mossy boots
like he's just this very forenoon
                wandered down the brae –

a chapman peddling bracken-besoms,
lichen-saucers
              a few lampwicks of grass –

I open the door, though he gives no hawker's cry –
just proffers his mute wares,
                  as he has for long enough.

Deliverance

I'm waiting for the star to rise
– a planet maybe

that every evening tangles itself
in the still leafless branches

of the sycamore
framed by your smallest window

where it seems to flutter and tremble
like thon pied wagtail,

mind? trapped in a lobster-creel
on the pier at Elgol.

O fisherman's hand, reach in!
Send us chirruping!

The View

For too long I haven't
         glanced at the sea
                 fully ten minutes!
– horizon shining like a magic key,
a whinny of spume at the cliff-foot,

      and all the sky's silences, its dialects . . .

Now here comes a squall
             all dressed in drab
bustling toward the mainland –
a smudge of rainbow
        clutched like a shopping bag
                 in her right hand.

Corporation Road I

One night, in my father's arms
I was carried from our brick-built semi,
shown the stars above the steelworks' glare.

Corporation Road II

On my red swing I swept
high as its iron
chains allowed, the sky

I rushed toward disdained
to gather me; I birded up,
dizzied by its blue, its ungovernable clouds –

come back, said the Earth
I have your shadow.

Eyrie II

That wind again, fit to flay you –
               like pages snatched
                   clouds flit west,
with all that's written there, heartfelt, raw –
The street-lamps sift their small light down
               on a wakeful street,
a slate slips, wheelie-bins coup
       and three fields away, a branch
on a Scots pine snaps,
       and down falls cradle and all.

What will the osprey do then, poor things
when they make it home?

Build it up, sticks and twigs –
          big a new ane.

Soledades

Having lost my copy of Machado's *Soledades*, I search the garden. It's March,
blustery, daffodils nod, and already blossom's sprigging on next door's pear.
I've a hunch I left the book by the old railway sleeper that serves as a bench,
and further, that the same breeze as makes the frogspawn quiver
in our sandpit-turned-pond, as flaps the laundry, has snatched the book away.
And sure enough, it's there, tossed beneath the beech hedge and open
at a particular page, as though the breeze, riffling through, had spotted
his own name among the master's lines:
                            The deepest words
of the wise man teach us
                        the same as the whistle of the wind . . .

The Glen

April morning, rising mist,
     last fugitive snow-drifts
cooried below the dykes' north sides,
       a naked mountain
ash tree next a tumbling burn —
Ay, it's a different season here, different world . . .

So if you don't mind, heather of the hillside,
and it's alright by you, small invincible bird,
I'll lean on this here boulder
     by the old drove road,
and get my eye in, lighting on this and that.

'It's nothing to us' you might shrug,
— and you'd be right.

Wings Over New York

One of the Central Park
　　　　　red-tailed hawks is
hunched in a leafless maple
pecking at a polythene bag.
When it flies its talons
　　　　　entangle in the plastic
　　　so it plunges head down
　　　　　– dreadful winged pendulum –
and everyone gasps,
　　　but with three strong wingbeats
it frees itself and soars
　　　　　(Where they nestin'? someone asks,
I heard on Dakota, this year)
above the American Natural History Museum.

At the pondside hop hermit thrush,
fox- and swamp-sparrow
　　　and elsewhere in the Ramble
sounds a tiny NYPD siren
　　　　　– a starling, high in a red oak.

Arbour

A sea-side arbour, a garden shanty,
knocked together out of driftwood and furnished
with a beat-up sofa
              is where I sit,
striving to cultivate the strandline's

take-it-or-leave-it attitude, and happy to remain
till the last young blackbird
                   flies the nest
lodged in the dog-rose to my left.

From time to time father bird
hops across our common square of grass,
                      cocking his head.
Friend, it's the sea you hear, vast and just
beyond those dunes, beyond your blackbird's ken,

but what do I know? May is again pegged out
across the whole northern hemisphere, and today
is my birthday. Sudden hailstones sting
this provisional asylum. We are not done yet.

Blossom

There's this life and no hereafter –
　　　　　I'm sure of that
but still I dither, waiting
for my laggard soul
to leap at the world's touch.

How many May dawns
　　　　　have I slept right through,
the trees courageous with blossom?
Let me number them . . .

I shall be weighed in the balance
　　　　　and found wanting.
I shall reckon for less
　　　　　than an apple pip.

The Hinds

Walking in a waking dream
I watched nineteen deer
pour from ridge to glen-floor,
then each in turn leap,
leap the new-raised
peat-dark burn. This
was the distaff side;
hinds at their ease, alive
to lands held on long lease
in their animal minds,
and filing through a breach
in a never-mended dyke,
the herd flowed up over
heather-slopes to scree
where they stopped, and turned to stare,
the foremost with a queenly air
as though to say: *'Aren't we*
the bonniest companie?
Come to me,
You'll be happy, but never go home.'

Ben Lomond

Thae laddies in the Celtic shirts,
                              a baker's dozen
lumbering all the way to the summit cairn
the hot last Saturday of May
                    as larks trilled
and the loch-side braes released their midgies . . .

Well, up at the raven-haunted trig-point
(as the sun shone bright o'er the whole lower Clyde)
they unfurled a banner,
and triumphant-sombre, ranked themselves behind it
                                for the photies,
    'R.I.P.' it read, then the name of a wee boy

they'll never meet again. Ach,
would the wean were playing fit-ba
          on some bonny banks somewhere . . .

There's no accounting for it, is there?
                    I mean the low road, and the high.

The Sheilings

Meeting no living creature
till the upper glen, where a few hinds
bounded away, I pitched my tent
on the emerald knoll
of a mossed-over sheiling hut. As the west-
facing hills dandied in the gloaming
and shadows filled the defiles, I fancied
I could hear the lasses of lang syne
ca'ing their kye, clattering pans, an infant's wail,
but the only sound was the Allt Ball a Mhulinn's
sweet-talk, which deepened
like a lover's, through the night.
What though, in June, is a night?
For a while the sky brooded, and once
a plane passed, high, heading south.

Solstice I

A late boat draws a wake upstream.
                    A 90s anthem
— stadium rock — pulses from a neighbour's window,

while four or five gardens down
                the reek of a bonfire rises
toward an overcast sky, dimming now
                but for an amber swathe miles long,
west-north-west above the Sidlaws.

Daylight's at full reach, and still has business here,
or so it thinks —
              but the town's swifts are hid
                    under their mysterious eaves
and it's gey near midnight. Then it's over —
midsummer: one fewer of our portion,
                        one less left in the jar.

The Cliff

Let's take our chances here with the mortal,
                the common and the mortal,
and stroll among the clifftop
                  drifts of pink thrift,
the throat-catching fulmar-shit updraft
and let space open
                between word and world
                    wind-strummed, trembling

The Stair

Nana you are not there, no
hale in body behind the black door but
here I come coiling up the stair wi my paper
poke of Jujubes and the *Beezer*. Two landings

first then yours. I dart whippit-quick
past the toilet at the turn
in case there's an auld
                          bogeyman hiding. Stone

gassy smell and it's twenty odd
                          years since the war, but
naebody's bothered to scrape the black-out paint
off the stair-heid window. Oh this was a bleak land then.

Nana will you not be there
                          in the room and kitchen?
Here's my fingernail, scratching a peephole to keek through.

The Girls

A summer evening,
                 a rubber ball
thumped against a harled
1950s gable wall

– and pitched between
chant and song,
our lasses' rhyme: *plainy, clappy,
roll-a-pin* – as we practised

birling round so quick
we caught the same ball
bingo! on its rebound – alive

to its arc and Earth's spin
as the gloaming deepened
and one by one, we were called in.

The Missing

When the wee girl toddled round the corner
                          into our street,
we quit our hidey-seek
and hunkered level with her
oddly drooping eyes. She was no one's
                          baby sister that we knew.
Was she crying? Maybe. Anyhow
her pants were soaked, so we pulled them off,
left them in the gutter, tugged down her yellow frock,

then gripping a small hand each, me and Sandra McQueen
set off with her,
                  back toward McColl's and the Co-op
– where else could she have wandered from?

Big girls, we knew the way
                      or so we thought
but the road, in its summer haze,
only seemed to lengthen, lengthen, lengthen, the more we walked.

World Tree

What kind of a tree was yon, stationed
like a beggar at the bottom of our lane
where we braved on scooters and wee bikes?

It marked our world's end, maimed,
relic-grey, down past the last back gate
where the fields began,
growing from before they built the scheme.

That was where we hunkered,
from infancy till the gloamings of our teens,
knees drawn up to our chins, whispering
sweet horrors . . .
                  Crone-tree, tribal-root,
I haven't thought of you in years, your sap
in me, but wonder now what kind you were
– elder or hawthorn, bour or may
                  – and why I suddenly care.

Fianuis

Well, friend, we're here again,
        sauntering the last half-mile to the land's frayed end
to find what's laid on for us, strewn across the turf –
gull feathers, bleached shells,
                    a whole bull seal, bone-dry,
knackered from the rut
(we knock on his leathern head, but no one's home).

Change, change – that's what the terns scream
                    down at their seaward rocks
fleet clouds and salt kiss –
everything else is provisional,
              us and all our works.
I guess that's why we like it here.
          Listen: a brief lull,
              a rock pipit's seed-small notes.

Migratory I

Mind that swan? The whooper we found
neck slack on the turf, head pointing north like a way-sign,
how you stooped and opened its wing?
                                        I paid scant heed
to your naming of parts: *coverts, ulna, primaries*
being scunnert with the place, its gales and sea-roar
– but this wing – this was a proclamation!
The wind-fit, quartz-bright power of the thing! A radiant gate
one could open and slip through . . .
We dragged the swan to the lee of an old dyke
tucked it in neat,   a white stone,
then trudged up out of the glen. At the ridge
again, we got clouted properly,
                        staggered on, half elated, half scared.

The Berries

When she came for me
through the ford, came for me
through running water
I was oxter-deep in a bramble-grove
glutting on wild fruit. Soon
we were climbing the same
sour gorge the river fled, fall
by noiseless fall. I mind
a wizened oak
cleaving the rock it grew from,
and once, a raptor's mewl.
Days passed – or what passed for days,
and just as I'd put the whole misadventure
down to something I ate,
she leapt twice, thrice, my sick
head spun, and here we were:
a vast glen ringed by snow-peaks,
sashaying grass, a scented breeze,
and winding its way toward us
that same world-river –
its lush banks grazed by horses, horses
I knew she'd leave me for,
right there, her own kin –
no use my pleas, no use
my stumbling back down
to where the berries grew,
because this is what I wanted,
so all I could do was brace myself
and loosen my grip from her mane.

Migratory II

eftir Hölderlin

As the burds gang faur
he luiks aye aheid
the prince o them, and caller

agin his breist
blaws aa he meets wi
i the heich,
        the quate o the lift

but ablo, his braw lands
lie bienly shinin

– and flittin wi him: hauflins
ettlin for the furst time
tae win furrit

but wi cannie wing-straiks,
he lowns thaim

Migratory III

Those swans out there at the centre of the loch
                              a dozen or thirteen
moored close together, none adrift –
                    they've only just arrived
an arrow-true, close-flocked, ocean-crossing skein,

and bone-weary, sleep now
                                        heads under wings,
so darkness can restore them,
though darkness is what they've just flown.

None today is the Watcher, none the Vigilant One,
                    scanning the rushes of the shore
for a few notes of movement,
                    a fox, say, or a lad they recall
thousands of years ago
                    skulking in a skin boat with his broken flute
and pockets filled with sling-stones.

Homespun

The yellow-shaded lamp
                squat on a table
in our mother's corner of the living-room
was made by us, from an empty
Dimple whisky bottle
                meshed in faux-gold wire,
and crowded to the neck with dog whelks or buckies
picked up from the beach at –
                                was it Brodick?
I can feel yet the itch of the green/
brown-flecked hand-knit I wore
                rapt on that seashore
                                gathering shell after shell.
What happened to that
                – the lamp, and all the stitch-work
it shone upon
                squandering no light?

Scotland's Splendour

At the back of our local charity shop's
a book I last recall
crammed into my bedside cabinet
among the *Beano* annuals and the *Broons*.
Its cover photo shows a river
racing from snow-crisped hills,
a bridge, a whitewashed byre,
scenery so familiar I open it,
and rediscover in 'full natural colour'
page after page of mountains
mirrored in placid lochs,
cattle ambling by reedy lochs,
stags on heather-moor
and one modern silver cataract:
the spillway of a new-built hydro dam.
All this, I'd been given to understand,
was 'Scotland', a gift sent down
during our sojourn among the southron
but too young to read, I'd simply
pored over its rowan-trees,
cottages, castle-crowned rocks,
hen-wives wearing woollen coats,
ferry boats in the gloaming. How odd
to feel its weight once more,
that hardback nation
which declared itself in our speech
– ours were the grey-rain tones of Clyde-built

trams and cranes (illustrated on p19)
— a dream-tinged land we pick up,
then shelve again, a place
so difficult and faraway
I grat miserable tears the day
my folks announced we were flitting,
turning north again,
back to thon unknown cold stone 'home'.

Wings Over Scotland

Glenogil Estate: poisoned buzzard (Carbofuran).

No prosecution.

Millden Estate: poisoned buzzard (Alphachloralose).

No prosecution.

Millden Estate: poisoned golden eagle 'Alma' (Carbofuran).

No prosecution.

Glenogil Estate: poisoned white-tailed eagle '89' (Carbofuran).

No prosecution.

'Nr Noranside': poisoned red kite (Carbofuran).

No prosecution.

Glenogil Estate: poisoned buzzard (Chloralose).

No prosecution.

Glenogil Estate: poisoned pigeon bait (Carbofuran).

No prosecution.

Millden Estate: shot buzzard.

No prosecution.

Rottal & Tarabuckle Estate: dead kestrel inside
     crow cage trap.   **No prosecution.**

'Nr Bridgend': remains of buzzard found under a rock.
     Suspicious death.

'Nr Noranside': remains of buzzard found beside
     pheasant pen. Suspicious death.

Millden Estate: satellite-tagged golden eagle caught
     in spring trap, then apparently uplifted
     overnight and dumped on Deeside.

No prosecution.

Glen Esk: Disappearance of sat-tagged red kite.
     No other transmissions or sightings of bird.

The Tradition

For years I wandered hill and moor
Half looking for the road
Winding into fairyland
Where that blacksmith kept a forge

Who'd heat red hot the dragging links
That bound me to the past,
Then, with one almighty hammer-blow
Unfetter me at last.

Older now, I know nor fee
Nor anvil breaks those chains
And the wild ways we think we walk
Just bring us here again.

Another You

That Sixties song on the radio tonight
shrank me right down
eye-level with the raffia-faced,
Bush-made wireless
hunkered on the sideboard
in our family semi. If I could
spell out its Old World names,
backlit with a wartime glow:
Moscow, *Oslo*, *Berlin*,
it's because you'd taught me:
holding up flash-cards
with   *LOOK   LOOK,*
printed in cheerful font,
making me sound out loud
the OO, then the Kuh
that stood, also, for *Kathleen*,
and the only song I ever
heard you sing – Joseph Locke's
'I'll take you home again, Kathleen'
which aye made me greet. Well
that old Seekers thing
sure took me home again:
Dad's chair, sofa, ornaments,
your knitting bag, all
needles and pins. Sometimes
I tried on your specs,
the ones kept among the yarn

and reserved for 'close work'.
Wearing them sent my look-or-seek
haywire: the sideboard loped,
the carpet yawed,
– but you'd snatch them back,
claiming I'd ruin my eyes.
'Close work' was your pride;
you'd steered the satin
of your own wedding dress
under the Singer's clamped-down foot;
our grey school jerseys purled
onto your lap. Even I had my uses:
hands outstretched, I'd tension
skeins of wool for you to wind;
and grew, as I grew, to relish
the brush of your inch-tape
against my skin,
arms-length was as close as we got.
But I was wee and loved
the wireless's valves'
hot-dust smell, the steam-iron,
gas-fire; warmly clad we were,
if rarely hugged –
love was a primary seven
dance dress you sewed for weeks,
a florid pinafore I wore
but once, then took scissors to –
not in malice, more in hope
that I too might magic
some transformation, from girlish frock

to the longed-for elegance
of a maxi skirt — a crime,
when you discovered it,
I couldn't explain. I never
could explain myself, never
could explain. But that old number
swelling through my kitchen
this dark November night
moves me dearly. It's seven years
since you died, and suddenly I know
what the singers say is true —
that seek as I might, I'll never
find another you. But that's alright.

Solstice II

Here comes the sun
                summiting the headland – pow!
straight through the windows of the 10.19
– and here's us passengers,
                splendid and blinking
                      like we're all re-born,
remade exactly, and just where we left off:
the students, the toddler, the tattoo'd lass,
the half dozen roustabouts
                    headed off-shore
                          cracking more beers and more jokes.
Angus at midwinter
                  or near as makes no odds –
faint shadows raxed
over fields of dour earth,

every fairmer's fenceposts
                  splashed with gold.

Gale

Whit seek ye here?
There's noucht hid i' wir skelly lums
bar jaikies'nests.

Notes and Acknowledgements

Many magazines, journals and anthologies offered first publication to the poems in this book. Among them, over the years, are: *Penguin Modern Poets*, *The Bloomsbury Anthology of New Scottish Writing*, *Times Literary Supplement*, *London Review of Books*, *New Statesman & Society*, *Poetry Review*, *Edinburgh Review*, the *Guardian*, *Poetry London*, *Chapman*, *Orion*, the *New Yorker*, *Columbia* (USA), *Landfall* (New Zealand), *Irish Pages*, *Irish Review*, *Irish Times*. My thanks to all the editors.

The Autonomous Region was originally a collaboration of poems and photographs from Tibet with Sean Mayne Smith. I thank Sean for the adventure.

Many of the poems have been broadcast on BBC Radio. The sequence 'Ultrasound' is part of a longer work commissioned by BBC Radio 4. 'The Glass-hulled Boat' was commissioned by Radio 3's Poetry Proms series. At the BBC, I thank Tim Dee in particular.

'The Wishing Tree' was written for the King's Singers, and performed at the Proms 2002, to music by Joby Talbot. 'Hoard' was commissioned by Salisbury Festival. 'Lucky Bag' was commissioned by the National Museum of Scotland.

David Constantine's fine translations of Hölderlin (Bloodaxe Books, 1990) formed the basis of several of the versions in Scots.

The Bonniest Companie began with a week's residency at Sweeny's Bothy on the Isle of Eigg. Many thanks to the Bothy Project.

A merle is a blackbird. In 'The Hinds' I was thinking of the last verses of the old ballad 'Tam Lin', when the Queen of the Fairies rages against Janet, saying: 'She has ta'en awa the bonniest knight/in a' my companie.'

In 'World Tree', bour-tree is Scots for elder, may is hawthorn. 'Fianuis' (say fee-ah-nish) is the north-running peninsula on the Hebridean island of North Rona. 'Migratory II' is a fragment by Friedrich Hölderlin. 'Migratory III' concerns Paleolithic flutes, 40,000 years old, made from swans' bones. 'Wings Over Scotland' is a 'found' poem, alas. https://raptorpersecutionscotland.wordpress.com/

'The Shielings' was written to acknowledge the 2015 Mark Ogle Award. A version of 'The Glen' was commissioned by the Bristol Festival of Ideas as part of their New Lyrical Ballads project.

In my decades of writing poetry, I've received valuable support from The Scottish Arts Council, Creative Scotland and the Paul Hamlyn Foundation. For this I am very grateful.

I'm truly indebted to Tom Fenton of the Salamander Press, and to Neil Astley of Bloodaxe Books.

I tip my hat to Don Paterson.